Seven Secrets
of the
Celtic
Spirit

"THE CELTS INVENTED THE HORSESHOE, which changed the way people traveled and worked and spent their leisure. They were the first to mine salt and market salt, which changed the way people lived. George Bernard Shaw said, 'An Irishman's imagination never leaves him alone.' Father Fitzgerald's imagination is clearly a second cousin to his craft. He writes like an angel and provides a masterful and poetic account of the Celtic spirit. His words light up a page and the reader is moved from fireworks to starlight over and over again. He has clearly inherited the spirit of storytelling. He is a gifted 'seanachie' weaving the history of the Celtic spirit through the pages of this book. Like Saint Patrick who picked a shamrock to show the Celts that the spirit of God was not somewhere above the clouds, but right there at their feet, right beside them at every moment, Father Fitzgerald shows his readers the same. Father William Fitzgerald has become the caretaker of the Celtic spirit in America."

—Pat McDonough
Psychologist, author, and columnist

"FATHER WILLIAM FITZGERALD'S BOOK, *Seven Secrets of the Celtic Spirit*, read prayerfully and meditatively, is a rewarding experience. The delightful stories, poetry and insights enrich the mind as well as the soul, no matter what one's ethnic background. I am happy to recommend it."

—Most Rev. Anthony M. Milone
Bishop of Great Falls-Billings, Montana

Seven Secrets of the Celtic Spirit

A Journey to the Soul of Ireland

William John Fitzgerald

ThomasMore®
– An RCL Company –
Allen, Texas

Acknowledgments

Scripture quotes from New Revised Standard Version, copyright 1989, Division of Christian Education of the National Council of Churches of Christ in the United States of America. Used by permission. All rights reserved.

Send all inquiries to:
Thomas More® Publishing
An RCL Company
200 East Bethany Drive
Allen, Texas 75002-3804

Telephone: 800-264-0368 / 972-390-6300
Fax: 800-688-8356 / 972-390-6560

Visit us at: **www.thomasmore.com**
Customer Service E-mail: **cservice@rcl-enterprises.com**

Printed in the United States of America

Library of Congress Control Number: 2001 135473

7479   ISBN 0-88347-479-4

1 2 3 4 5   05 04 03 02 01

Dedication

For my sister Mary Rose

And all my beloved cousins
and dear friends
who have taken her place.

Acknowledgments:
Robert Reilly, Susan Gallagher,
Dolores Whelan, Jeannie Beal,
Peggie Deegan, Barbara Bachumas,
Father Liam Treacy, Father Pat Smith,
Mimi Robertson, Kerri O'Brien,
and Gladys Leach

Contents

Introduction

As I sat in Bewley's Coffee House in Dublin, I glanced out the window onto Grafton Street where throngs of people swirled by. This street scene could have been in Brussels, or even Stockholm, for northern European people pretty much dress the same and most have fair skin not touched too much by the sun. What was unique about this thronging crowd was their youth. Dublin is a young city and Ireland is a republic where the young are the majority. Yet I had come to Ireland to search for something ancient—the "Celtic Spirit." So I turned from gazing out the window, poured some cream in my tea, and recalled recent conversations I had enjoyed over coffee with Dubliners—Michael, Fiona, and Molly.

I had remarked to them, "You know, seeing all these vibrant young people in Ireland makes me wonder about the ancient 'Celtic Spirit.' I would like to believe, for instance, that one of the secrets of the Celts is a kinship with the natural world. Their ancestors had an almost mystical connection with nature, and with the animals, birds, and sea creatures who were their fellow travelers and often their teachers. Do these modern young people passing by, who are at the cutting edge of the cyber world, still hold on to any of the ancient Irish and Celtic spirit?"

Michael was quick to respond: "Ancient spirituality? Not the young ones—not much anymore. They have a new spirit and a new God—money! They are losing everything from the past. They want to be 'European,' not Irish. They now even blame the church for everything—even for the scars from British colonialism. Exhibit A—if you need one—Sinead O'Connor!"

As Michael spoke, Fiona held her peace, her cigarette smoke curling around her like some kind of aura. Fiona, with the dark brown flashing eyes, was twenty-seven. Michael, beginning to gray, was the elder—fifty-six years of age—old by Irish standards and Molly a grandmother at fifty. After Michael's strong words, there was a long silence. Fiona finally spoke up: "I don't agree with Michael at all. The kinship with nature—the 'Celtic Spirit' as you call it—it's in our bones. And it's in the bones of the young people you see throngin' the streets. They may not talk to you about spirituality, nor be in church as much as before—but the spirit—oh yes, we have it."

Then I turned to Molly and asked her, "Molly, let me ask you a different question. Is there something special about the Irish spirit—and, if so, what is it?"

There was a long pause and then she answered, "Well, ya know, I can't say—because it's all in my heart."

Finally, Fiona spoke again. "Well, if you want to find that spirit, and you think kinship with other creatures is a part of it, go out around the country, and I guarantee you'll find it."

And so I did. I have journeyed seven times through Ireland. Each time brought adventure and an unfolding of new personal insights. I have summarized my own personal experience in this book by proposing seven secrets that I have discovered. Are there more than these seven? Of course! And if one were to travel there a hundred times the journeyer would never exhaust the hundreds of subtleties of Ireland's unique Celtic Spirit.

It just may be possible that visitors from another land can sometimes glimpse specks of sparkling gold in the cultural stream of a foreign land. And some of the inhabitants who live there might take this gold for granted or even miss it. This might be true of visitors to Ireland where the Irish people have been going through a transition from an almost theocratic state to a modern secular nation whose horizons have been enlarged by entrance into the European community.

This is not meant to be a scholarly tome. There are many of those and they speak well of the Celtic Spirit. Rather, this book is anecdotal. It contains experiences illustrating how the Celtic Spirit has weaved its way through my own personal life journey—and not just in Ireland. For it also has enriched the fabric of my life through my own Irish American experience here in the U.S.A.

Each chapter in this book begins with a poem, for this is the Celtic way. The book also contains imaginative stories, for this also is the Irish mode. My own experience suggests seven "secrets." Seven is a holy number. I began to discover these secrets for myself in 1973 on my ascent up Croagh Patrick Mountain in County Mayo. The pilgrimage path up this holy mountain has been carved out of holy ground, first by the Druids, later by Saint Patrick, and then by the Christians of the last 1,500 years! So this holy mountain is a fitting place to begin a search for Celtic secrets.

Seven Secrets

But why call the insights in this book "secrets"? Because there are certain ancient insights that have too often been neglected. Or they have even been shoved out of the way by our ever accelerating techno culture and current postmodern values. These secrets are worth rediscovering in our times, certainly in the United States and the Western world. They may even be worthy of rediscovery by some of the natives of Ireland itself. In the new century, a serious reappraisal of religion is going on now in Ireland and some have become alienated from church structures, which, in their view, were unable or unwilling to deal with a variety of serious problems. At the close of the twentieth century, Thomas Cahill wrote a landmark book, *How the Irish Saved Civilization*. At the beginning of the twenty-first century Mary Kenny wrote another: *Goodbye to Catholic Ireland—How the Irish Lost the Civilization They Created!* In it she gives an even-handed appraisal of this possible loss. In her reassessment, it appears that twenty-first-century Irish generations who rush to form a secular nation may lose sight of some of the great spiritual treasures that are their ancient heritage—making what was evident in the past—secrets in the future.

In the following chapters I attempt to point out divergences between our hyper, postmodern culture and the ancient Celtic worldview and suggest we would do well to integrate some of the older Celtic Spirit into the rushed and busy lives we live in our Western consumer societies. At the end of each chapter, there is a special meditative prayer with a suggestion for journaling. So I invite you to join me on a journey to the soul of Ireland.

Prologue

Croagh Patrick

O nce upon a time, in a thin place beyond time, I had a dream. Looking out the window I saw a brown polluted haze dimming and damning the sun. Across the way a river flowed filled with garbage and bereft of life. Beneath my window snarled traffic and squealing tires and the road rage shouts of red-faced drivers. And yet beneath it all, or beyond it all, from the riverside came the faint tapping of two hundred dancing feet. Its staccato chorus seemed to tap out: Celtic Spirit! Celtic Spirit! Celtic Spirit!

And when I left the window and tried to read, over and over, poets and storytellers kept referring to Celtic Spirit, and to the renaissance of Celtic Spirit. And sometimes for a few moments I would think I had grasped Celtic Spirit but then it would be gone. So where was Celtic Spirit to be found and held? How should I know it? How might I have it?

Would that I could find this Celtic Spirit for all my hours! And time passed and the day darkened. The night fell upon the suffering earth and still I longed for this elusive Celtic Spirit. I stood by the window and searched the starlit sky for Celtic Spirit. I prayed for Celtic Spirit. Then amazingly from the distant sky I saw an object hurtling toward me. As it took shape, I was startled. It was an ancient fiery chariot pulled by two white horses, their manes furling out, and their eyes wild and exuberant. And standing with the reins was a beautiful raven-haired woman. Upon her shoulders an emerald woolen cloak—broached together by a golden spiral clasp. "I am Brigid, Bride of the Gaels and keeper of the fire, come with me and I will take you to Celtic Spirit!" And so, I climbed aboard and we hurtled through the skies, above the clouds toward the stars and ever eastward.

At the edge of dawn, in the faint pre-light, an island appeared below, quilted with patchwork fields and farms and down, down we went to the foot of a mountain where the horses pulled up, held back by Brigid's firm hand. "We are here," she said. "This is the holy mountain Croagh Patrick *(pronounced crow)* in the County Mayo. And this is a thin time and a thin place where time matters not and the spirit world is very close."

Brigid took from her chariot a shepherd's staff and we alighted. She touched a rock and a fire sprung up. "Look here by the rock, this is the memorial that will lead us on the path toward Celtic Spirit." Sure enough, there stood a sculpture of starving people on an ugly coffin ship and an inscription, "In Memory of the Famine."

Then, out of the dark stepped a monk. His head was shaved in front, but his hair was full behind. On his shoulder sat a beautiful white dove and at his side stood a remarkable longhaired hound. "This is Colmcille, also known as 'The Dove,' announced Brigid. "He is the sacred scribe of Erin and he will write down for you seven secrets of Celtic Spirit." Colmcille then said, "In ancient times, we fasted and prayed and suffered severe penances—for us the white martyrdom, since in the sixth century we were not granted the privilege of the red martyrdom. But over the centuries this island has pursued an heroic quest, a great adventure, that in the first millennium sent brave Brendan into the setting sun and her missionaries to the rising sun—into Europe when the flame of faith needed to be rekindled. But for the last millennium the adventure has been here within this island, which was to be drenched in blood, suffering, famine, and sorrow—and its people blessed with long endurance. So I write for you on this scroll a first secret of the "Celtic Spirit" and it has three parts. In golden script, he writes: **The Holy Three—Heroic Adventure, Compassion, and Hospitality.**

Now the hound bounds toward the mountain and the dove takes flight behind. With her staff, Brigid points forward and announces, "Let's go forth now on a grand adventure ourselves. There are six more stations, where Celtic Spirit may be revealed, but they can only be reached by an arduous climb up this holy mountain. So Colmcille and I fall in behind her. We can smell the heather and the gorse as we wind our way up a gentle slope. At the end of the slope, we stop. Again, Brigid strikes a fire and Colmcille says, "My great hound Liam and my namesake—the Dove—are reminders that the Celts value the ancient wisdom of those creatures who were here long before humankind. And then he writes on the scroll, **The Blessing Path—Through Sacred Water and Over Holy Ground.** "This," he says, "is the second secret of the Celtic Spirit."

And Brigid replies, "Yes, to walk with reverence upon the sacred earth—this is a lesson Celtic Spirit has to teach your new millennium. And when we do that, the earth blesses us; when you do not, there is a curse upon the land and the future children who spring up from an earth that is poisoned. This is why your time and your place needs to catch the Celtic Spirit—to breathe clean air, to fish in living streams, to grow from unpoisoned soil.

And now we continue on. We are still in the dark, for there is only the faintest hint of the coming dawn. After climbing for a while on a steeper grade, we pause and Brigid brings forth fire with her holy staff and Colmcille now writes upon the scroll the third secret: **Kinship with the Natural World—Especially Animals, Birds, and Sea Creatures.**

We begin to climb again and the path becomes more rocky and uneven. And now the first pink light of dawn brightens the eastern sky, and down below to the left of our path on a cliff edge we can see breaking surf and, glancing back, a green carpet covers the shaded valleys. The climb is rockier and steeper.

Brigid stops, lifts up her staff, and points to the four directions: "Beauty all around!" she proclaims. And Colmcille writes upon his scroll, what we are feeling, the fourth secret of the Celtic Spirit: **Enchantment and Allurement.**

I ask Colmcille to talk a little about enchantment. He responds, "Enchantment comes when the eye is awed and does more than look—and the heart knows more than meets the eye! An enchanted heart sees deeper and even further than the beauty around us. An enchanted heart expects coincidences, fortuitous events. and knows that the space is very thin tween this world and the next. Enchantment demands wonder and awe and openness. It expects wondrous surprises. Some in your time call these eruptions of unexpected energies. Other wise persons speak of amazing grace, still others providence. The Celtic heart has always known that there are spirits and unseen forces at work all around us. There are thin times and places. What we see is not all we get. Your physicists are now discovering this with their probing minds—a mysterious, dancing order of being beneath the surface of all things. The Celtic heart has always known that enchantment brings magic and mystery and it feeds the spirit. And for the Celts, enchantment is all around!"

We resume our climb now and we can hear the waves breaking below. The climb becomes more and more steep as we make our way toward the reek's high brow. Up, up, farther as the sun now breaks up over the sea. Somewhat breathless, we pause again. Brigid rests her staff. "Let us praise God with the morning sun! We praise you, God of the long hand who lifts up the fiery ball of the sun and hurls it over our heads! We praise you, O God, whose allurement attracts the running tides! And we praise you our God who paints the holy earth in every shade of fertile green. Bless the old sod beneath our feet for it is our precious holy land!"

And Colmcille shouts, "Amen!"

"Come now, the hardest part of this journey is about to begin." Indeed. The path narrows and steepens, for we are approaching the crown of this holy mountain. Before us now, we see a steep incline and it is nothing but loose shale; there is really no spot firm enough for a path to be established. The last ascent will need to be on our hands and knees! So we pause and rest.

And I proclaim, "I have a great thirst!"

Brigid answers, "Don't we all! I should like to have a great lake of ale for the King of Kings. I should like the whole of the Heavenly Host to be drinking it for all eternity! But we are on pilgrimage here and thirsty we shall be! And now, Colmcille, would you be revealin' the fifth secret?"

And Colmcille unfolds the scroll again and writes upon it the fifth secret of the Celtic Spirit: **Storytelling and Good Humor.**

"For the Celts there is a story to be woven around all life's events. Where the salmon leaps, there lies a story. Where the spring gushes forth, there is a story—so that all of life is woven together with meaning. And the Spirit weaves the warp and the weft of our tales. So wherever the Celts gather there will be laughter, poetry, and storytelling. It is our gift. And just as long-suffering is one of our traits so too laughter in the midst of tears is our heritage. They shall know us by our stories and we shall come to know ourselves and the workings of the mysterious Spirit in the telling of our tales. And often laughter is the child of Celtic storytelling."

Again we resume the climb. It is steeper and steeper, and a little out of breath, we pause again and Colmcille unfolds the scroll and says, "The sixth secret is: **The Beauty of the Poetic Word and Creative Imagination.** We have always been night people; the dark is a holy place of fertile incubation. Our ancient poets knew well that the creative spirits dwelled in the holy darkness. This is why they secluded themselves in darkened 'Houses of Memory' to learn the sacred poet's role. For us Celts, the poet's place was of equal honor to that of the warrior."

And now, Brigid lifts her staff and points to the mountaintop. "Listen," she says. "Can you hear that?" And sure enough, there is a rhythm drifting down from the mountaintop. "Celtic Spirit!

Celtic Spirit! Around and round with Celtic Spirit!" And Brigid says, "We will follow the sound, follow the beat, follow the music—but we must crawl to get there, and so we do, up over the loose shale, slipping and sliding, grasping for something solid. The great hound Liam bounds before us and the white dove flies high and disappears beyond the edge of the mountain's crest.

We are now within reach of the very top. Breathless, we pause. Brigid says, "The seventh secret of Celtic Spirit you will see in a moment on the flat space atop this peak. And where we will find it is in the holy circle." Now we are almost there. And looming up above the edge is a high cross—the cross with the circle around its arms and now we peek over the edge and behold a wondrous sight. There is Saint Patrick smiling, dressed in a kilt, amid people dancing in a joyful circle, but not just people; there are lambs skipping, rabbits leaping, Liam too lopes around the circle, and above Colmcille's dove and other birds circle all around and there in the very center—dancing the Resurrection Dance: Jesus himself.

"Oh yes!" says Colmcille. "Now you know the seventh secret of the Celtic Spirit. And he writes on the unfurled scroll: **The Holy Circle—The Dance Around the Celtic Cross.** This means faith conceitedness, or kinship. In the Holy Circle of Life we dance the Resurrection Dance!"

And then Brigid looks very stern and says, "This is the scroll and the message you are to take back with you to your polluted and overheated world: Heal the sacred circle. Mend the fractured earth! Clean the polluted waters! Show compassion in the sacred circle, and new life shall rise again. Take with you the breath of Celtic Spirit and breathe the fresh air of life—not the stench of death."

CHAPTER ONE

The Holy Three—Heroic Adventure, Compassion, and Hospitality

The First Secret of the Celtic Spirit

The Cliffs of Moher

A garland on rock's brow
Does the rock soften?
Might we plant flowers
at the sharp edges of our lives
between rocks and hard places?
Would our craggy cliffs
be easier seen?
Yet more inviting to climb?
Plant the flower of adventure,
the fleur-de-lis.
Plant the flower of passion,
the Red Rose of Tralee.
Plant the flower of hospitality,
the mistletoe green.
Plant flowers
at the rough edges of life.

M ost recently, when I stood at the edge of the Cliffs of Moher in County Clare, and spotted daisies clinging to the precipice, it stirred the poet in me as it must have stirred poets going back through the mists of history. I can only imagine how the Cliffs of Moher have stirred all the generations of the Irish. For when you stand at the edge of this precipice, the great stone face of the reddish cliff drops straight down into the Atlantic. And here the birds fly not above but way below, arching around the jutting rocks and skimming over the breaking waves.

This cliff of sheer rock is the very western edge of Europe itself. It is a boundary space. The Celts valued boundary spaces and often saw them as opening into mystery and other worlds. Looking out from here, the next land site is North America. So the ocean horizon beyond the cliffs is the beckoning edge of new worlds and promised lands. History shows that so many of the Irish people have reached beyond this horizon to plant their seeds at rough edges and in fertile places. And the venturing forth from this edge for so many has been a saga of heroic adventure.

The First Secret

I believe it may have been at the Cliffs of Moher that I began my search for the first secret of the ancient Celtic Spirit and identified it for myself as the heroic quest for adventure. I could imagine the "coffin ships" of the nineteenth century delivering the immigrants from the jaws of famine but also onto a dangerous adventure. Many of them would never reach North America. Weakened by the famine, and confined in horribly close quarters, they died at sea. Their only consolation was the compassion and hospitality shown by relatives and friends. So when I thought of their adventure it seemed to me this heroic quest for adventure also had two daughters—compassion and hospitality. This holy threesome, adventure, compassion, and hospitality, are historically Irish traits. And the number "three" for the Celts has always been a sacred number.

Journeys

When we consider our own personal lives, most of us will thankfully never know such a dramatic venture as the journeys of the coffin ships, but there are journeys we make that challenge our sense of compassion and hospitality. Some of these may be only as far as from our car to a sick room. There are other longer journeys. Some take us to college or to the service, or to unsought job relocations. These journeys may open the door to homesickness. As the plaintiff Irish folk lyric proclaims: "When the leaving's over . . . the leaving's just begun."

SEVEN SECRETS OF THE CELTIC SPIRIT

However, through such journeys the long arm of the unknown future reaches out and tugs us forward toward adventure and new challenges. There are unknown companions "out there" who will need our companionship, and our compassion, just as we will need their hospitality.

A trip means making the quickest time with the least bother. A journey will contain surprises, unexpected detours, and delights and will always challenge and test the journeyer. A journey means traveling with a light heart into the unknown beyond the horizon.

My Seven Journeys to Ireland

All of my seven goings to Ireland have been journeys, not trips. About twelve years ago, I was planning to go over to Ireland and explore Irish folklore in out-of-the-way places. The tour was named "Journey to the Soul of Ireland" and was to be led by Dolores Whelan, director of "Education for Changing Times" in Dundalk, and Sally O'Reilly, two learned Irish women who were trying to rediscover some of the secrets of the feminine role in ancient Celtic Spirituality.

Since I knew we were going to be on the move climbing fences and slogging through pastures, I thought it would be a good idea to go over a few days early and rest up at the seaside in preparation for the very active tour. I obtained the name of a retreat house on the ocean near Dublin. I called their number and a woman answered. I explained to her about the tour I was taking and my desire to find a restful place for a few days before getting into the tour.

There was a hesitation and then she said, "Well, you know you can't be stayin' here because they are all closed down. They are all away on holiday. I don't work here at all. I was just passin' through to return a book."

And I responded, "Oh!"

There was another pause and then she said, "Ah, you sound disappointed. Well, why don't you give me your name and your number and I'll look around here and see if I can find you a place where you might stay."

At this point, this person in Ireland knew nothing about me, not my name, my vocation, or anything else. Yet, she signed on immediately to be my helper in finding a place to stay! After that, we exchanged names—me, "Father Fitz," and her, "Mary."

"All right," she said, "I'll be callin' you tomorrow."

The next day, she did call and announced to me, "I come into the parish house every day and leave an evening meal for the priest, and he's goin' off to Lourdes with a group. There's no reason you can't be stayin at his place, and he agrees so it's all set."

I was amazed at her calm voice that held within it so much efficiency and hospitality!

"So, what time will you be getting in and where are you comin' in?"

"I will be coming in at Dublin at eight o'clock on Tuesday."

"Well I can't get there at eight." She replied. "The young one (she had several children) is just startin' school that day, and I have to take him at eight. I'll come and pick you up at ten. How's that?"

"Well, that is just fine, Mary."

"OK, what do you look like?"

And so it came to pass. She picked me up and took me to her priest's house. After getting in, she said, "Now, if there are some places you'd like to see during the day, with the young one now in school, I could take you around."

And so she did. One of her favorite places was the leaping waterfall at Powerscourt in the Wicklow hills which I had never even heard of before and is now one of my favorite sites too.

The second day when she came to take me on another outing, I opened the conversation by asking, "Well, Mary, what's the program for today?"

She laughed heartily and responded, "Ah, you Yanks and your programs! There is no program over here!"

And so began a friendship that spans an ocean and twelve years. And every time since when I go to Ireland, Mary and I get together at least for tea if we possibly can. On a recent journey, I took my cousin Rosemary and our friend Donna, and we spent an afternoon with Mary driving through the Wicklow hills. It was wonderful for us and a break for Mary who now with her children full grown was a full-time hospice nurse for the dying priest who had been so generous to let me stay in his quarters.

That hospitality many years ago in a very real way smoothed over the tiny "rough edges" of disappointment. Mary is a person who plants flowers at the rough edges of life, not just for me but for a lot of others as well. That trip to Ireland may not have been an heroic quest for me but it was an adventure that was open to surprises. And it allowed me to discover the deep and genuine hospitality that so often is found in the Irish people.

When we examine the history of Ireland we discover the adventurous spirit along with long suffering, compassion, and hospitality which are often the daughters of hardship. Too often in our postmodern culture the most dramatic adventure we are familiar with are the vicarious ones we view on our TV and movie screens. One of the secrets we need to learn in our wired and programmed world is the secret of real life adventure, and the compassion and hospitality that can grow from it. Perhaps compassion can only be learned by those who have suffered immensely. If this is the case, then compassion comes easy to the Celts since they have suffered much over all the centuries.

Origins of Adventure, Compassion, and Hospitality

Where does this Irish sense of adventure, compassion, and hospitality come from? Only sociologists and historians can adequately answer that question, but we might make our own guess at it by quickly skimming the pages of history and doing a thumbnail summary. J.C. Beckett, in his *A Short History of Ireland*, describes six epochs of Irish history. We might consider how adventure, hospitality, and compassion had their own six epochs in Irish history.

The First Period—
The Heroes and Heroines of Old

The first period would be that of the ancient mythic heroes and heroines. Cuchulainn who sleeps three days and nights while his soul takes flight, Queen Maeve, the warrior Goddess, and all the rest. They performed mighty deeds and were immortalized by the poetic bards. In those pagan times, the living even provided hospitality to the dead at certain thin times and places. The seeds of the Celtic Spirit were buried deep in that Druid and pagan time.

The Second Period—
The Era of Saints and Scholars

The second period is that glorious time from approximately A.D. 500 to 1000 when Ireland became known as the "Land of Saints and Scholars"—when the Irish missionaries took the place of the earlier pagan adventurers and tramped eastward over the byways of Europe following their hero, Jesus Christ. And early in that era Brendan the Navigator journeyed west beyond the Cliffs of Moher and the horizon in search of a promised land of saints by the setting sun. There was adventure enough in those exciting days. And since the wandering Irish monks needed to receive hospitality in far-off places, they in turn never ceased to provide it to the wayfarers who traveled by their houses.

We also find an ancient Celtic practice of fosterage—that is, children from one community or tribe were fostered out as children to spend some time with another family or mentor. This was a great act of trust on the part of the parents "lending the child" and of hospitality of the fostering receptors. Saint Brendan himself was fostered to another woman, Saint Ita. So not only did the child receive hospitality from infancy, the child in his or her earliest years began life with an adventure beyond the usual familial boundaries.

The value of hospitality was even enshrined in the Celtic Brehon law code. As early as the fifth century persons in authority were to welcome unexpected guests to their tables with no questions asked. In most homes there was always room for any uninvited guest.

The Third Period—The Dark Age

The third period might be called the dark age of trial and persecution—an adventure in long suffering. For 800 years, the Irish struggled against invaders and knew various degrees of persecution. Even as late as the seventeenth century when the Anglo Irish (English colonists planted in Ireland) had brought English influence to a part of Ireland called "The Pale," an English scribe, writing of those "beyond the pale," would report to the king: "There be more than sixty counties called regions in Ireland inhabited by the king's Irish enemies . . . where reigneth more than sixty captains . . . that liveth by the sword and obeyth no temporal person."

A little later under Queen Elizabeth, this Irish defiance of the English invader was mostly quashed. And it appeared that at last the Anglo Irish, settlers from England, would finally remake the Irish people into proper English subjects. And what law itself would not accomplish, in 1649 the invader Oliver Cromwell would attempt to finish with the sword and torch. This effort would culminate in the eighteenth-century English penal laws which were a concentrated effort to wipe out the Celtic culture, language, and Catholic religion and make the native Irish second-class citizens. It also deprived native Catholics the right to obtain any land either by purchase or inheritance. For the Irish people this was an adventure in travail and survival. Hospitality in that era meant hiding priests in "priest holes" in the ground so they could escape the penal law which in its harshest years decreed death by drawing and quartering for any popish priest caught having Mass for the people.

The Fourth Period—Near Death

A fourth period might be called a time of near death and near extinction and it lasted from the seventeenth century unto the twentieth century. It was an era of lost battles and quashed risings. And in 1845 the famine struck. In that fateful year many of the Irish began to scatter across the world. For some their adventure on "coffin ships" meant death before they could ever reach landfall. For those who did reach America, they often saw signs in store fronts reading "No Irish need apply." So leaving a beloved homeland and settling in a strange place challenged them to be hospitable to later arrivals.

The immigration for all the strangers from foreign lands was one of the great adventures of history. On the dock at Cobh, I stood and looked at the green hills along the shore. That was probably the last scene my ancestors remembered of Ireland. Next to me there was a lovely statue of fourteen-year-old Annie Moore and her two younger siblings. I could imagine these children with their bundles taking one last look at Ireland before walking up the gangplank and into a grand adventure. They sailed over to the New World in 1892, arriving in New York on Annie's fifteenth birthday and she turned out to be the first immigrant to be welcomed at the brand-new Ellis Island. Like Saint Brendan before her, she symbolizes the Irish adventure into the West beyond. In the next decades, 580,000 other Irish would follow her. Back in their former homeland, many of those who remained endured grinding poverty and the scars still left from the famine.

The Fifth Period — Resurrection

If the nineteenth century was a century of near death, the twentieth was a new fifth period that ushered in resurrection. Almost 800 years of trial and subjection reached its finality in the 1916 Easter Rising in Dublin led for the most part by teachers and poets! And something surprising also happened. By the time of the Rising, some of the descendants of the Anglo Irish had become more Irish than British, just as my Norman ancestors, the Fitzgeralds, had become during previous centuries of colonization. When it came time to reclaim the ancient Celtic Spirit and rise up, William Butler Yeats, an Anglo Irishman, not only explored the ancient Celtic lore but he also immortalized the Easter Rising in poetry by proclaiming that "a terrible beauty is born!"

And another Protestant, Anglo Irish patriot and heroine Constance (Booth) Markewicz—holsters on her hips—would lead a column in the 1916 fight against the British army at Stephens Green in Dublin. When the Rising was put down, Constance was sentenced to death but later pardoned by the English Crown for fear of international uproar over the execution of a woman. But there was no mercy shown to most of the other leaders of the Rising. When they were executed one by one, the tide for a subjected people turned, and freedom for twenty-six counties of the island was eventually won but only after a final bloody civil war.

The Sixth Period—Transformation

The turn of the twentieth century into our new millennium found the descendants of the last century's immigrants as highly successful citizens in their adopted lands. Over forty million Americans claim some degree of Irish ancestry! The election of John Kennedy as president forty years before the turn of the century finalized their arrival in a new land and the full integration of the Irish into the American scene.

The turning of the new century also marked a real transformation in their ancestral homeland. In our most recent time, the Irish people in the old country have outpaced even their former colonial masters and most of Europe in economic growth. For the first time in centuries her sons and daughters were not her major export. Instead they were staying home and riding the "Celtic Tiger" of a burgeoning economy.

In this new century there is a vibrant Celtic revival through music, dance, writing, and motion picture arts that is being exported throughout the world. There is in Ireland today an explosive reenergizing of Celtic culture and folklore. Cahill's *How The Irish Saved Civilization* has explained the roots of this transformation. "River Dance" has brought it from the head to the toes and Irish writers have made the short story their genre. This is a time when an Irish poet, Seamus Heaney, faithful to an ancient Celtic love of the poetic word, would receive the Nobel Prize. All of this reveals for the whole world to see the latent and powerful Celtic Spirit sometimes hidden, but always passed down through all the epochs. Through all the years it is a tale of adventure, compassion, and hospitality.

The Panorama of History

Looking at the panorama of these historical developments, it would seem that every age brought with it new challenges for adventure. Sometimes it was the adventure of going out, venturing beyond the comfortable horizon. Other times adventure meant holding on and surviving, and sometimes it meant rising up. In almost all of the times it often meant suffering much. And perhaps only those who have suffered much can feel deeply the need of compassion for others who suffer and the need to welcome and provide hospice for other weary travelers on famine and persecution roads. Finally, in our own time there is a dynamic transformation, the flowering from all the seeds of two millennia. And the Irish have remembered their history and have been quick to provide help in Africa where famine too often stalks.

Over Coffee—Asking the Irish about Hospitality and Adventure

Perhaps there are other simpler, homely reasons why people like Mary and so many Celts exemplify such a wonderful sense of compassion and hospitality. I searched for these over coffee in conversations with Mick and Tricia from Clare. And for the Irish sense of adventure, I spoke with a mentor of mine, one of the most knowledgeable of Americans in Irish ways, the writer Robert Reilly.

When I asked Tricia about the Celtic Spirit and the reasons for their wonderful hospitality, she answered, "Well, maybe you don't have to look any further than the hearth! The Irish women I knew from childhood had an innate sense of service, of accommodating, of making things right. And when the times were tough, like alcoholism in the family, they were strong and held things together—not always codependent—but strong. They were never flunkies! You know we had a neighbor spinster woman who would come in to help my mother. She was there for us in all of my childhood. But we had no word for 'maid.' She was a valued person who was there to make things better. As I remember, I think all Irish women were brought up to be kind. They would never define themselves as 'strong,' but they were. Yes, when you talk about the Celtic Spirit and hospitality, I think that the Irish women I knew were born with it."

Mick added to this by saying, "You know we live on an island, not a continent. And often in close quarters. I think all of that has helped us to develop a certain civility toward one another, which is an element of hospitality. You might find grudges among us. Someone once said, 'Irish Alzheimer's means forgetting everything but your grudges!'—But you don't find very much rudeness. We live shoulder to shoulder so in some very basic sense we make room for one another. I think that has a lot to do with hospitality."

Adventure

When I visited with Robert Reilly about the Holy Threesome—Adventure, Compassion, and Hospitality, he responded, "If you want to start with Irish adventure, get in touch with the Navigatio—an account of the voyage of Saint Brendan the Navigator in the sixth century. This allegorical tale was well known in the ninth century and there are remaining copies. It describes an epic journey westward out of Ireland by Saint Brendan and a company of his monks. It is very interesting that Christopher Columbus made a journey to Galway before he ever sailed westward and very likely may have been drawn there to check out the story of Brendan."

Very interesting indeed! The saga of Saint Brendan begins in the year A.D. 484 when he was baptized at a holy well in County Kerry. Early on he was fostered to Saint Ita, a woman mystic. He would live for almost a century, dying at the age of ninety-three! In all of those years, his travels and his influence spread far and wide—starting from his birthplace on the north shore of Tralee Bay, County Kerry. From his crib he could smell the sea. His later travels extended to Scotland, Wales, and Brittany. His influence and his story was well known in medieval Europe. Some estimate that the monastic houses he founded had as many as 3,000 monks. Clonfert, close to the River Shannon in Galway, was a monastery founded by Brendan in A.D. 550. He is buried there and it has been a place of pilgrimage for centuries.

Brendan is forever linked to the sea and the rivers that flow into it. From his long and adventurous life, today's historians are most interested in the journey he describes in his *Navagatio*. In this tale, the journeyers are searching for "The Promised Land of the Saints." This long epic tale is really a compilation of many journeys taken at different times. What especially interests today's historians is the part of the *Navagatio* that seems to agree with a route that would go northwestward through the Faroe Islands up to Iceland, past Greenland and down to Newfoundland. Although told in poetic language, there are references to an island filled with birds which resembles the Faroes. Brendan also called the largest of the "Faeroes," the "Island of Sheep." And indeed "Faeroes" means sheep. Even today, the islanders have a Brandon Creek which local folklore holds was the embarkation point for Brendan and his monks. He also describes a very friendly encounter with a whale. Later on Brendan describes being "pelterd with flaming, foul smelling rocks" which could have happened in Iceland, the land of thermal hot springs and ancient volcanic activity. There is also a reference later to "towering crystals" which is not too bad a description of the icebergs they would have encountered near Greenland.

A current scholar describing the text of the *Navagatio* points out that, had Brendan been writing a pious tale, he would have brought in divine intervention. It is not there and so the text has the feel of a poetic but historic account of a real journey. If it was, it means that Brendan and his monks reached North America centuries before the Vikings and Columbus.

Is there any evidence for such an arrival? In 1976, Tim Severin constructed a "curragh" boat from primitive material, a wood frame structure covered with animal skins as close as could be imagined to the curragh Brendan would have sailed. He successfully sailed this boat on the Ireland-Faroes-Iceland-Greenland arc, making landfall in Newfoundland. This does not prove that Brendan sailed this route but it does establish that it was possible for him to have sailed it successfully in the sixth century.

Brendan in America?

Archeologists are now paying more attention to ancient stone remains found at Salem New Hampshire as well as Grotan in Connecticut and others even in West Virginia! Some of these remains near Salem only eighteen miles from the ocean are corbel structures very similar to ancient corbelled structures in Galway. Besides this, they have discovered etchings on some of the stones, which seem to be written in Ogham, an ancient Celtic script known by Brendan, as well as Chi Rho's with a distinctive loop identical to some in Galway.

The Chi Rho

If these hardy and adventurous monks did arrive in the New World in such an ancient time, the Chi Rho carved in stone tells why they came and whom they served. Jesus Christ took the place of the ancient Celtic heroes and heroines in the days when Erin became the land of saints and scholars. They recognized him as a hero who lived a life of adventure. He seized their hearts and their spirits.

Centuries later, when the Irish rose up in the Easter Rising, one of the martyrs executed by the crown was the hero and poet Joseph Mary Plunkett. Perhaps no one has written more beautifully about Jesus as the wellspring of the Celtic Spirit, He expresses in a lyrical way how his ancient forebears saw the cosmic Jesus in all of nature and how they saw Jesus possessing a strong hero's heart.

I see his blood upon the rose
and in the stars the glory of his eyes.
His body gleams amid eternal snows.
His tears fall from the skies.

I see his face in every flower.
The thunder and the singing of the birds
are but his voice
and carven by his power
rocks are his written words.

All pathways by his feet are worn.
His strong heart stirs the ever beating sea.
His crown of thorns is twined with every thorn.
His Cross is every tree.

Joseph Mary Plunkett, "I See His Blood Upon the Rose"

A current prominent scripture scholar, John Dominic Crossan, has written a memoir, *A Long Way from Tipperary — What a Former Irish Monk Discovered in His Search for the Truth*. It may be that the thirst for adventure that he describes as his primary motive for entering into monastic life was also a very real call for the ancient Irish monks — an adventure following in the steps of their hero, Jesus Christ. Crossan writes: "The foreign mission meant adventure. . . . God clearly had the best game in town, the most exciting game around."

The postmodern world of the twenty-first century is also a post-Cold War and post-World Wars time frame. Perhaps we have lost track of heroes or heroines involved in great adventures, or have we? It sometimes seems that the anti-hero has replaced the hero. At this writing, two of the most watched TV spectacles would be professional wrestling, where the bad guys are now the stars, and the *Survivor* episodes. *Survivor* which drew forty million viewers for one episode, featured cutthroat competition and the survival of the fittest, who just happened to be the meanest.

At the turn of the new century, writers had to turn the clock back to find the great heroes and heroines who emerged in World War II. So, has the heroic adventure and its daughters, compassion and hospitality, disappeared from the postmodern culture? Not really.

Carl Jung in "Two Essays on Analytical Psychology" writes about the need for heroic adventure by ordinary people. He indicates that there are hidden heroes and heroines all around us in our everyday experience. In order to fulfill our everyday demands, we are all sometimes challenged to a heroism that cannot be seen from the outside. And if this call for heroism in everyday life is not engaged or fulfilled, Jung writes, these ignored opportunities can actually lead to neurosis.

Hidden Heroes and Heroines

Interestingly, Jung claims that hidden heroism is a normal asset for leading a healthy life! And there are heroes and heroines all around us. They are as diverse as the spouse taking care of a mate with Alzheimer's, the volunteer fire fighter, a parent patiently and wisely dealing with teenagers, the recovering alcoholic, the teacher willing to take a low-paying teaching job when she (or he) could make so much more in another field. Among the heroic are so many of the sick who bear their burdens with grace and patience. None of them would consider themselves as heroes or heroines on some grand adventure. But they are.

Heroic and Adventurous Irish Women

Tricia's comments about Irish women also hold true. Brendan was a hero of the sea. Irish mothers were often heroines of the hearth. And so many of their daughters ventured forth on heroic quests. These Irish immigrant maidens sailed in Brendan's wake—far away to new lands. Many worked as housemaids in America. They had difficult, low-paying jobs, yet they sent home what they could to their impoverished relatives. They also contributed mightily to the growth of the church in the New World. One historian remarked that the contributions of Irish housemaids and nannies built Saint Patrick's Cathedral in New York City. If they indeed built the cathedral it was their religious sisters who were pioneers in creating Catholic schools and health care. They all brought with them adventurous spirits, deep compassion, and traditional Irish hospitality. And so many were successful at planting seeds at the rough edges of life. Such stalwart Irish women faced difficult odds in a new land. Overcoming those odds demanded heroic efforts.

Compassion

What all the everyday heroes and heroines have in common in any age is that they go up against difficult odds. There are other oppressed people who only have the energies to attempt to survive. These deserve more than our sympathy, or empathy. Compassion is more. It is a passion for justice, for mercy, for making things right for those without the power to do so themselves.

We see this passion in the lives of the saints and so many Irish missionaries of every age who chose Christ as their hero and then brought the adventurous Christ, the hero with the flashing eyes, into the lives they touched. This was the passionate Jesus who overturned the money changers' tables and fed the hungry. When we examine the lives of the Celtic saints we discover them to be passionate people following their hero Jesus and willing to take risks and journey far on the hero and heroine's trail.

Hospitality

The third of the holy threesome is hospitality. It would seem that in our accelerating culture the odds are stacked against hospitality. We build houses without porches, garages in front, no sidewalks in front, no alleys in back. In the past porches provided opportunities for interaction with neighbors and alleys places for kids to play. Many people drive out of their garages in the morning, back in at night without ever sighting a neighbor or stepping on the earth. Can anyone say that the suburbs are conducive to neighborliness? Many do not even have sidewalks that can lead us to hospitality.

We are also so often glued to our cell phones that our conversations keep being interrupted and we are never really present to anyone. In our culture, genuine hospitality has become almost a heroic virtue. It takes quality time and we just have too many other things to do to take time to offer hospitality.

This may be why when we journey to Ireland we are stunned and amazed at the warm hospitality. There is a lesson to be learned here. The first of the "Seven Secrets of the Celtic Spirit," the triad of Heroic Adventure, Compassion, and Hospitality, we need to return to all our lives.

Prayer

Jesus — Heroic Sailor,
you calmed the tempest on the sea.
In my life's adventure,
be before me as I set my course,
around me in all life's storms.
Brendan — navigator,
guide me past the shoals
and through the needle's eye.
Inspire compassion and hospitality
for those adrift on life's seas.

Journal Option:
For me, the healing adventure . . .

CHAPTER TWO

The Blessing Path Through Sacred Water and Over Holy Ground

The Second Secret of the Celtic Spirit

The Poem of Amergin,
as he set his right foot upon Eire

I am the wind which breathes upon the sea,
I am the wave of the ocean,
I am the murmur of the billows,
I am the ox of the seven combats,
I am the vulture upon the rocks,
I am a beam of the sun,
I am the fairest of plants,
I am the wild boar in valor,
I am a salmon in the water,
I am a lake in the plain,
I am a word of science,
I am the point of the lance in battle,
I am the God who created in the head the fire.
Who is it who throws light
into the meeting on the mountain?
Who announces the ages of the moon?
Who teaches the place where couches the sun?

A Human Blessing Path of 102 Years

He was remarkable! Imagine a man who lived in three centuries. Imagine Michael born December 31, 1899, in County Kerry in Ireland—still alive and well on January 1, 2001! As a child he had seen all deliveries by horse and wagon. In 1918, he had fought in the trenches of the "Great War." In the twenties, he saw a Civil War in his own land. In lean and hard times he got his degree and spent many a day lecturing on science in a college. He lived long enough to see another "Great War," in the bloodiest of all centuries—the twentieth. And he lived to see humans land on the moon, and to become aware more than anyone in previous centuries of the "Great Story"—the story of evolution and the forming of the universe! Now he was celebrating the new millennium and his third century!

He now sat before the turf fire, his shock of white hair glistening in the firelight. His face was a ruddy red and the winds of three centuries had carved lines there. His only deference to age was a tweed cap pulled down on his brow to keep away the draft. His eyes were mirthful and the fire danced in them.

As the turf fire glimmered, it cast a soft light on the faces of his great-great-grandchildren. The three of them sat at his feet in a semicircle of adoration. The oldest, eleven-year-old Sean, piped up: "We're your great-great-grandchildren, aren't we?"

"Oh, you are indeed!" the old man replied.

Sean smiled beneath a shock of red hair and replied, "That's even grander than our folks—us bein' double great! Well then, tell us a great story, Grandda, our "seanachie"! *(pronounce: shahn-ah-kee)*

And then Bridgid the youngest squealed, "Yes! And tell us an old, old story!"

"Sure'n I will—the oldest of all stories," said the great and grand old patriarch. "And may the stillness be upon your thoughts and quiet be your tongues! For I tell you a tale that was told at the beginning, the one story worth telling!"

The old man took in a deep breath and began to spin his tale. His voice was clear but soft-spoken now after the wear and tear of a century. "Well, now, this story I'll be after tellin' you has something from the old days, the time of the Druids and even before. It has something from the time of the saints, and some things I learned late in life from my mentor, Thomas Berry, who called his book *The Great Work*. So here is my tellin' of this old and great story:

"Some say that before there was anything else our lovely Ireland existed because in all our ancient lore we have no Irish creation myth. But Thomas Berry sees it differently and it's his way I'll be tellin'. Once upon a time, there was only the holy dark. That's where you started, ya know, within your mam in a dark and holy place. But long ago before there were any mams or das, it was very dark everywhere. Then something stirred in the dark. Suddenly light flashed and sparkled and like one great lightning strike bits and pieces flew out from the center and flew through the sky and lo and behold they formed into balls which kept expanding."

"Oooh!" they murmured. "You mean like when we blow up our soccer ball?" said Bridgid.

"Yes, dear child, but these were large balls, some as large as our earth and some larger. And among them all there was only one, as far as we know, that was after a long time clothed in a beautiful green and blue. And on that blue and green ball—I'll tell you a secret that not everyone knows—one island was greener than all!"

"That's no secret to us, Grandda—it's our dear old sod, isn't it?" said Patrick.

"Yes, Pat, the fact is our dear old sod is the greenest of them all. And as an old seanachie told it to me—from the holy sea and from this sacred sod came forth animals and birds but they could not see, you know, for there was not enough light. So the deer caught their antlers in the hedgerows. So our dear earth needed light, And so, Lugh, God with the long hand hurled a fiery ball into the sky and called it "Sun"! And then he threw a curve like a soccer ball caught by the wind—a companion to the earth who would soften the nights and make lovers' hearts tremble."

"The moon!" they all cried.

"But, Grandda, you said there were no mams nor pas then! After the sun and the moon, and the animals, how long was it before mams and daddies came?"

"Ah, that is another secret that we never knew till now. Listen now! One hundred fifty million years ago!"

"Oooh!"

"Yes, indeed. And all of these creatures who came before us were primal blessings because they were so beautiful. In fact, the long hand of Lugh pointed at them and said: "They are all very good!" Since they were here 150 million years before our kind came, the animals and birds were learning so much about living on this lovely earth so they could teach the first mams and pas a lot about how to live here."

"What did they teach the first mas and das?"

"Oh, the wolves and the dogs taught us humans to be loyal to our clan just as they were to their pack. And the salmon taught humans not to give up, to keep leaping and to keep trying.

"Many of the mas and das learned good things from the animals, and the birds, and the plants, but some refused to learn. In fact, some refuse to learn even today.

"Time went along and many of the mas and the das got bigger and bigger. Too big for their britches! The old storytellers tell us, I can't be sure of this, but it is said that some came to be giants. They wanted to be bigger than anyone else. And these giants built a bridge of perfect hexagons between Patrick's Head at the top of Ireland all the way to Scotland. But then, lo and behold, a big flood came and they and their fancy bridges were washed away! But that flood was not the BIGGEST flood of all. That came long before."

"When was that?" asked Patrick

"Well, you remember Noah and the ark. Well Noah's grand-daughter Cessair got a tip from her grandda that the biggest flood of all was going to come. It's wise to listen to grandda, you see. So Cessair and many of her women friends and just several men set sail and traveled westward toward Ireland. And they were the first people to reach Ireland. Did the flood reach Ireland? We don't know. If it did, they would have some fine mountains to climb. Mount Brandon would be closest to where they landed. Now, my gassoons, let me ask you a question. Since this is an old, old, story, who was the first poet among our ancient ancestors to come to dear old Ireland?"

"I know! I know!" shouted Sean. "It was Amergin, son of Mil from whom all the Gaels descend!"

"Well, right you are, son! Tell me now, are they still teachin' you to recite poetry the way they did for us when I was young?"

"Oh yes!" said Sean.

"Well, can ya be tellin' me what his first words were when he set foot on our holy land?"

"Yes!" said Sean. "Can I quote them for you, Great-great-grandda?"

"Well, I would like that very much, Sean, for my old voice is wearin' a little thin and I'd like to put my tongue back in the barn for a little shelter now."

So Sean stood up proudly and this is what he proclaimed:

"As soon as he put his right foot upon our old sod, this is the song Amergin, son of Mil, sang—our first Gaelic poem, and these were his first words:

> I am the wind which breathes upon the sea,
> I am the wave of the ocean,
> I am the murmur of the billows. . . .

"Right now, that's all I can remember."

"Well, you've got the first words of it Sean. Well done. Do you suppose that Amergin knew in some way what scientists tell us today?"

"What?" they all asked.

"Well, that we are all one in some way with all the waters and lands. Water just keeps circulating around, you know, from the oceans back to the clouds and down again in blessed rain. And this water and the air too circulate in and out of us. Just think, little ones, some of the water you drank today may have been the same water that Amergin waded through, or that Blessed Patrick blessed the people with. Amergin followed a blessing path through the holy water before he stepped on the Holy Land. And, as for you, your blessed births came out of the water in your mamas' womb! And then your folks took you to church and you passed through water again when you were baptized. This is part of the secret that folks often forget: Our first blessing path is through holy water!

"Well, now, let me ask you what else happened after the great flood? Do you remember?

"I do!" cried Bridgid. "The rainbow!"

"Yes, indeed, the rainbow. The rainbow was a sign of God's love and care. It started at Mount Ararat when Noah's boat came to rest. But where did it go and where did it end? Ah, that is the mystery, isn't it?"

Then Patrick asked, "Where did Amergin and the rest of the early people in Ireland come from? Were they from close by?"

"Oh, not at all! There were five different invasions and they came from afar. Some say that the last group to come were the Tuatha De Danann. They brought many good things to our Ireland, for they were artistic. We've discovered many beautiful results of their craftsmanship. Later on, when Patrick came to tell us of the hero Christ, they took to the fields—not city folk, our fairies, and some took to the sea and became merrows—half seals and half humans. Some would say they were a curse on the land and the sea. But I don't think so. I think they make us more aware of the mystery of earth and sea. And what is mysterious reminds us that there is always more than meets the eye."

"But what about the rainbow? What was at the end of it?" persisted Bridgid.

"Oh, it's the rainbow that's got ya thinking, is it?"

"Oh, I know," said Sean, "—a pot of gold!"

"Ah, you've all been so good with your answers, you have, but you know I think the 'pot of gold' is only a symbol. It stands for something else. It stands for a great blessing."

Now the old man bent over and looked intently and said, "Here's the last part of the secret I'll be tellin' you. The 'pot of gold' is our precious old sod itself! I think the rainbow arched through the sky and landed right here in Erin. The very land upon which we stand is the pot of gold! So, dear children, walk softly upon it. Bless it and it will bless you. Think now, when God wanted to send the very best—he sent his Son whose body was fashioned from sacred earth. That is why another great poet who I knew so many years ago would write:

> I saw his blood upon the rose
> And in the stars the glory of his eyes.

"Ya know, it's a part of our Irish spirit to treasure and never disdain the earth. It is the great mother womb of all life. It is where the seed needs to fall so there can be new life. It is even the seedbed where the dead body of Jesus himself was planted! And it was from there that everlasting life sprang up! Ah, yes, the gold at the end of the rainbow! So live the secret, children. Sail a blessing path through the holy water and walk a blessing path upon the holy earth and the end of the rainbow shall be yours!"

Blessings Passed from the Old to the Young

Thus spoke the old storyteller. And in the telling the old wise one revealed the "speech of the people of heaven in his mouth." For he had lived his life well. In his story and his long life journey he very well fulfilled and deserved an ancient Lorica blessing going back to the ninth century:

> May the yoke of the Law of God be upon his shoulder,
> the coming of the Holy Spirit in these ears,
> the smelling of the Holy Spirit in this nose,
> the vision that the people of heaven have in these eyes,
> the speech of the people of heaven in this mouth,
> the work of the Church of God in these hands,
> the good of God and of the neighbor in these feet.
> May God dwell in his heart
> And this person belong entirely to God the Father.
> Lorica of Fursa, Ninth Century, "The Second Millennium Challenge"

The old man in his storytelling has indeed revealed a second Celtic secret—a blessing path through the sacred waters and over the holy ground. And this is an endangered truth in our twenty-first century. Our age needs to rediscover the ancient Celtic worldview—its sense of the sacred place upon which we stand. This second secret of the Celtic Spirit reveals the earth beneath our feet as a dear old friend—"the dear old sod!" It is this dear old sod which enlivens the Celtic sense of place.

Two experiences come to mind which illustrate how closely the Celtic Spirit is grounded in earthly places. We were in Killarney, about to drive the Ring of Kerry. When we told our hostess Helen about our upcoming journey around the Ring, she replied, "And why would ya be doin' that? There is no sense of you drivin' it yourself. That way the driver does not see much at all. Sure'n, a bus will be after pickin you up right here at the front door and relieve you of all the drivin'." And so it came to pass. The mid-size bus picked us up at our door and we were off on our trip around the Ring. However, before we got to the Ring, the driver announced that "Two Garmin girls are marooned off the road a wee bit, and sure'n, it would be grand if we picked them up." So off the main road we went and down a lane—a wee bit—which amounted to six kilometers!

And there they were, two German girls burdened down with knapsacks and a couple of maps which from the looks on their faces were no help at all. Not long after they boarded the bus it also became evident that they did not speak a word of English. Soon the driver pulled to a stop and began to shout directions over his shoulder to the two bewildered twenty somethings. And here is what he said, "Now, gorls, listen to me. Ya get off the bus here and walk straight ahead through the hedgerows. Keep walkin' next to the water. You'll pass some gorse and go around where the ducks are. Then pass through the gap and up the hill. Finally, when you reach the top, stand by the tree and a bus will pick you up."

Each and every direction was given not according to kilometers but rather according to landmarks. The girls looked bewildered and we all motioned to them it was time to leave the bus. As they disembarked, the driver realized finally that they had not understood a word he had said. He shook his head, and muttered, "Glory be to God, I'm afraid we'll never see those gorls again!" Later, as we continued our own trip, my cousin Rosemary would chuckle and say, "And do you suppose those poor "gorls" are yet standin' by the tree?"

Another Irishman recalled a time when he accompanied an Irish friend to London to look up the friend's Irish sister. When they arrived at the proper street and alighted from the bus, he asked his friend, "Now what is your cousin's street address?" The answer came, "Sure'n, I don't know exactly, but not to worry, I'll recognize the tree in front of the house!"

These two incidents reveal the Celtic sense of place that is anchored in their close relationship to the earth and its own language of direction. For them, directions came from the earth itself rather than from some map far removed from the rootedness of place. For them, the earth is a friend that speaks and gives its own directions!

The Primary Celtic Realization—A Sense of Place

It is precisely this relationship with the earth and the sacred waters that differentiates the ancient Celtic worldview from the modern information age. For the Celts, earth is a friend close at hand, an intimate who speaks! Creation itself is a "thou," not an "it." This is the primary realization that lies at the heart of the second secret of the Celtic Spirit. Patrick Pearse, who founded his school at Rathfarnham outside Dublin in 1910, wrote: "If our boys observe their *fellow citizens* of the grass and woods and water as wisely and lovingly as they should, I think they will learn much." Pearse believed that nature will speak its own words to us from the waters and from the land if we but listen.

What are the words she desires to whisper in our ear? Among them are:

endearment,
beauty,
Go slow. Gaze at me.
mystery,
poetry,
charm,
enchantment,
peace,
contemplation,
refreshment,
and renewal.

And of course she can also shout words of chaos and messiness like:

    volcano,
    hurricane,
    cyclone,
    as well as rain
    and wind.

And sometimes when we think we are in control of everything, Mount Saint Helens, or Aetna, or Montserrat shouts at us in rumble and fire: "Wake up! Be AWE-FILLED!" And often words like "wind" and "breath" speak to us of the majesty and power of God, as well as God's closeness, the mystery that is at the heart of all creation, "the Holy Wind"—the Holy Breath of the Spirit.

Awen

The voice of a fluid and feminine spirit also overflowed from the Druids into early Irish Christian times. They called this fluid and feminine spirit "Awen." The poet calls her forth from the sacred sea and she speaks words of inspiration. The bard proclaims:

> The Awen I sing,
> From the deep I bring it,
> A river where it flows.
> I know its extent,
> I know when it disappears,
> I know when it fills
> I know when it overflows.

This subtle "spirit of Awen" perhaps inspired the early Christian Celts to envision the Christian Spirit as a stream flowing through the believer as evidenced in this blessing prayer from *Carmina Gadelica,* a book of over one hundred Celtic blessings:

> The form of God is behind thee.
> The form of Christ is before thee.
> The Stream of the Spirit is through thee
> To succor and to aid thee.

Clifford Stevens writes that, for the ancient Celts, leaping water was the language of laughter, and laughter was the language of God. He calls this God speaking through natural reality—the very hovering of God. And Terrence Sheehy answers the question "What is it to be Irish?" by saying that being Irish means knowing the language of all living things. And of course both earth and water are the essential seedbeds of all living things.

The Earth Speaks
Through Her Writers

It is also the earth itself that speaks to us through our human stories and poems! More and more modern authors have their ears close to the earth. Very often they give voice to the suffering earth of our own day. Likewise, they often express a certain sense of our human place on the earth. Thus John Grisham's *The Painted House* has the dirt-poor cotton fields of Arkansas speak their piece. The Irish American writer Mary Gordon understands the Celtic root-edness in place when she titles her memoirs, *Seeing Through Places: Reflections on Geography and Identity*. Her book jacket describes her writings as "linked essays which help us to see how integral places are to the lessons we learn." And when we have this sense of place, we walk a blessed path of recollection.

The Jewish novelist Havdalah expresses the universal truth of contemplative reflection of the earth beautifully in his novel *The Hand Before the Eye*. One day, when the main character Farbman is pushing and tugging a pile of rocks in a field, he stops for a moment and removes himself from the dictates of time—thus mastering the art of not doing—but just being. The author tells us that Farbman "takes communion with a stand of oak trees." This is precisely how the earth spoke to Saint Colmcille in Derry's woods as well as to all the Druids before him: "Derry mine, my small oak grove, / Little cell, my home, my love!"

Sometimes in traveling through Ireland you might see a farmer simply standing still in a field. It may well be he is doing what Farbman did—stepping out of time and taking communion with the beauty all around him. Scott Russell Sanders writes about having a sense of being in a place that is beyond and deeper than just doing something at a place. He writes that we have to know where we are so that we may dwell in our place with a full heart.

Despite its multiple advantages, our information age has removed us from being in a place where we are able to hear the earth's primary speech. We are always mobile and on to the next place before we ever arrive in the first place! We have also climbed a tower of Babel. The ubiquitous cell phone, which is a blessing in emergencies, becomes an addictive curse in daily life. Plugged into so many moving ears, we try to be in two places at once rather than being grounded in the present moment and place. Perhaps the penultimate moment of cell phone abuse occurred recently when the ushers at our parish noticed a well-coifed woman returning from the distribution of Holy Communion while jabbering away on her cell phone!

Disconnection and Alienation

A disconnection from any grounding is symbolic of a deep and pervasive alienation—our separation from and disdain for the earth. Richard Anderson, a professor of environmental studies at the University of California at Santa Barbara, even goes so far as to say that "At the heart of the modern age is a core of grief." And he ascribes this grief as a natural and human reaction to the rapid decline of the natural world. When we think "dirt" we think "laundry." Or we think of "raw material" which we falsely consider limitless and which we can exploit as we please. Whereas most of our ancestors, when they thought "dirt," thought about fertility. And the Irish thought of a beloved old sod.

Perhaps the most vivid symbol of this "raw material" attitude is the destruction of the green rainforests which impact the climates of the entire world. In the last fifty years, 50 percent of the world's rainforests have disappeared, giving way to the roar of chainsaws and the quick profit of human despoilers.

The chain saws add their noise to the tower of Babel where we in the developed and "first world" enthrone ourselves on high like Humpty Dumptys. This tower of denial puts us far above and beyond the earth connections that are vital for health and well-being. There we are severed from the grounding that connects us to the spiritual and aesthetic energies that only the earth can supply. For after all, we are earthlings and to deny our earthiness is to lose our identity. At a cultural and artistic level, the novelist Tom Wolfe has shown us how far we can fall from our "masters of the universe" perch in his novel *Bonfire of the Vanities*.

At a spiritual level, an ex-playwright and spiritual leader who himself lived in two centuries, John Paul II, catalogued some of the abuses that threaten the integrity of all creation. In a World Day of Peace message in 1990, Pope John Paul II chose Saint Francis, who loved Mother Earth and Sister Moon, as the patron needed for our day. Among the abuses of our time he cited the disrespect for life that invites pollution, and the reckless exploitation of natural resources. He addressed the ecological crisis and pointed out that "Christians in particular realize that their responsibility within creation and their duty towards nature and the Creator are an *essential part of their faith.*"

"The Wearin' of the Green"

This old Irish folk song reminds us that "the shamrock is forbid by law to grow on Irish ground." The song harkens to the worst days of the penal laws when "They are hanging men and women there for the wearin' of the green."

Today this song can refer to the earth itself. In our own time shortsighted laws provide loopholes that enable environmental destruction, thus condemning the *earth* for the "wearin' of its green." Or, as our astronauts have observed from high up in space, global warming seems to enable green vegetation to begin to grow up in cold places, thus upsetting the balance of nature.

In some sense the experience of fertile Ireland and the Irish drama of the great famine might serve as a metaphor for the twenty-first century ecological crisis. On the one hand, Ireland has always been a penultimate example of green fertility. To fly above her is to glimpse every shade of green. Kissed by the Gulf Stream she gives life to palm trees in the south and rich grazing grounds in the north. And yet this island of abundance experienced the terrible potato blight that caused many to starve and multitudes to emigrate. The blight was a simple breaking of the ecological circle with horrible consequences.

Today, pesticides and other abuses of the soil threaten the earth's very womb of life. The blight came uninvited to Ireland but too often today humanity invites devastation for short-term profit and long-term degradation. There are several traditional "capital sins" of humanity that war against the "wearin' of the green." They are seldom mentioned today but they prevail far and wide. They are the ecological sins of gluttony, intemperance, and idolatry.

Gluttony and Intemperance

There is an old Irish folk saying: "Better a small portion with a blessing than a large portion with a cursing." These words are pertinent for the first world. The fact is that the industrial nations possess only one-fifth of the world's population and yet consume two-thirds of the world's resources. And this minority of the world's population generates 75 percent of the world's pollution and waste! E. F. Schumacher, in his book *Small Is Beautiful: Economics as If People Mattered*, argues that continued growth and development without any boundaries is a recipe for disaster. The ancient Celts had a keen awareness of boundaries in contrast to our postmodern view that "the sky is the limit." Schumacher writes that in the whole Christian tradition the cardinal virtues are essential for our times. In particular, he mentions "temperance" which gives us the wisdom of knowing "when enough is enough." And the poet, philosopher, farmer Wendell Berry claims that he knows of no American who is not contributing to the destruction of the earth!

A New Twenty-First Century Challenge

In the past, Christians fasted from food and drink. The twenty-first century, which has ushered in terrorism, demands a new form of fast. Seeking more fuel-efficient autos, car pooling, taking conservation seriously, would lessen our dependence on the volatile Middle East and become a spiritual as well as patriotic form of discipline. The new threat of terrorism will demand new sacrifices and new disciplines.

Idolatry

John F. Haught, another insightful author writing about ecology and eschatology, states: "Modernity unfortunately has not accepted the earth's obvious finitude, and this idolatrous attitude underlies the ecological crisis." Idolatry always involves putting some human creation in the place of God! By gazing down from our "Humpty Dumpty" tower and proclaiming ourselves the "masters of the universe" we act as though we can do anything we please with earth's resources. In doing so, we are playing God. Haught points out: "This universe . . . is God's creation and not our own. . . . If we truly hope for the complete unfolding of God's vision for the universe, we will take immense delight here and now in saving the natural world for the sake of its future in God."

Immense Delight

"Immense delight in saving the natural world!" This has indeed been the very warp and woof of the traditional Celtic relationship to the earth with its beautiful glens and forests, its streams and grazing lands. To walk a blessing path upon the earth and to sail with God through the holy waters requires a gratitude attitude. It is only when we sense the simple essentials of life as beautiful gifts to be treasured and conserved that we can genuinely be filled with delight. This is the energizing path of the Celtic saints. They saw all creation as gift and the gospel as gift for living. Consequently, they set out on many paths over hills and through glens to share their delight with God's creation and in God's Son, Jesus, who was of the earth. Isaiah's words fit them well:

> How beautiful upon the mountains
> are the feet of the messenger
> who announces peace,
> who brings good news. (Isaiah 52:7)

The Great Easter Vigil—Feast of Great Delight

Anne Clifford, C.S.J., in her article "Foundations for a Catholic Ecological Theology of God," suggests that the readings of the Easter Vigil call us to respect the earth. In those readings God is actively present in the world beginning with creation. Its imagery depicts God as continually bringing order out of chaos and breathing over troubled waters, thus sustaining and recreating life.

The Easter Vigil is also very significant in the journeys of Saint Patrick. Both of his two journeys to Ireland were made over very troubled waters. They were movements through chaos on the way to new life. And when he celebrated the Easter Vigil at Tara, that Easter feast became the gateway event for his evangelization of Ireland.

The Vigil— Through Holy Water onto Blessed Earth

The Easter Vigil might well be considered a microcosm of the blessing path through the sacred water and over the holy earth. All of the elements of a creation-centered and eco-friendly spirituality are to be found within it. At the Easter Saturday Vigil, in the dark of night, under the stars, new fire is struck from rock. The new fire flares up in the night and ignites the great Easter candle, the symbol of the Risen Christ emerging from his dark and earthy planting. From rock, to fire, to water, to words, which come last— the Easter procession moves and these basic earth elements are allowed to speak to our souls. It is only after walking the blessing path under the stars that the procession enters the church. So nature speaks first. Then come the first scriptural words from the Genesis creation account where God proclaims nature good.

After the candle has been incensed, the deacon breaks forth in the magnificent Easter *Exsultet* containing this paean to the beauty of our earth which shares the glory of the cosmic Christ:

> Rejoice, O earth in shining splendor,
> radiant in the brightness of your King!
> Christ has conquered! Glory fills you!
> Darkness vanishes forever!

And then an amazing and ancient fertility rite takes place in front of the altar! (In some sense it resembles the ancient Celtic ritual of a new king being wedded to the feminine earth!) The Christ candle is immersed in the Easter water symbolizing Christ having intercourse with the womb of Mother Church so that catechumens can be birthed as newly baptized children of the church! There is no other official rite so earthy! There is no other Christian rite that so reverences earthiness. There is no other rite so primordial which contains all the basic elements of creation—rock, earth, fire, wind, and water.

And then the catechumens step down into the Easter water, "buried with Christ in Baptism," and then out again, "so that [they] might rise with him to new life."

> On Spring's holy night,
> Full moon glowing
> primal waters, silver shining, still recall:
> Hebrews dancing through,
> long ago, yet ever new.
> Lively waters,
> the graceful sea,
> Parting, rippling, breaking, beckons:
> "Whales spouting! Dolphins cavorting!"
> "Catechumens!"
> "Join with us in dancing!"

The Easter procession path is the penultimate blessing path. And it is the path trod by the Celtic saints. Saint Patrick blazed the path in Ireland at the Easter Vigil! Ever since he lit the Easter fire on Tara's hill and confounded the Druids, the Celtic saints have walked a path that reverenced God's earthly creation. Like Joseph Mary Plunkett they saw Christ's face in every flower, his cross in every tree. And they saw his light in all the stars that shone upon their blessed path. As the great Easter *Exjultet* proclaims:

> May the morning star
> which never sets find this flame still burning.
> Christ that morning Star
> who came back from the dead
> And shed his peaceful light on all mankind.

For the Christian Celts, Christ and the flowing Holy Spirit suffused the cosmos and in some very real way fulfilled the poetic imagery of Amergin. The Easter Vigil identifies us with both Jesus Christ and the earth itself.

Prayer

The Holy Land of Ireland!
Mount Brandon broods
above sloping comrade mountains.
Great slate cliffs drop down to the sea.
The sacred waters share abundance.
Whales, dolphins, fishes,
speak the voice of the ocean.

Skellig Michael juts up.
A rock skull with delicate
tonsure of vegetation.
So small its garden.
So powerful its prayer.
Hedge rows like a jumbled rosary.
The earth prays its every bead.
May I pray and act for:
fertile earth and abundant seas.
And rejoice in my earthy essence.

Journal Option:
**For me, a holy journey upon the holy earth and
a passage through the sacred sea brings to mind . . .**

CHAPTER THREE

Kinship with the Natural World — Especially Animals, Birds, and Sea Creatures

The Third Secret of the Celtic Spirit

With swift pace
increasing speed
dolphins leap.
Sheep dogs scurry.
Horses vault and press on.
The Sacred Crane returns to Erin.
And in their grunting, barking, soaring,
All creation gives God praise!

In slower pace
contemplative gait
a farmer walks.
His milk cows amble,
their hips swaying and tilting.
On the road, they form a lyric picture.
Framed by hedgerows and misty mountains.
All are one. One is all.

Go to rural Ireland and you will find the Irish walking a blessing path with other creatures. Often they walk with a dog at their side and other creatures before them. Meander through rural Ireland and you will often notice the attitude of farmers and shepherds toward the animal and sea creatures. They would seem to value them as more than just products for consumption. Rather they are most often treated as fellow inhabitants of the green earth possessing a dignity of their own. And so the third secret of the Celtic Spirit is kinship with the natural world, especially with animals, birds, and sea creatures.

In his novel *Banyon Tree*, the Irish writer Christopher Nolan elaborates not just the attitudes of the humans in the story, but also the sensitivity of the pony who pulls their cart. Nolan webs a tale of kinship of humans with the animals and with the soil.

The Runt

So here is another Irish story about such kinship. It begins as all stories do—once upon a time:

The pint of Guinness stood alone on the mahogany bar, its foam "drawing." Sean McCarthy's gnarled hand rested beside it, waiting. At his side sat his old friend Dr. Michael Garrahan. Breaking the silence, Doc asked, "And, Sean, what have you to say about Sunday's match?"

"Ah sure there will be some scalps taken!" But surprisingly Sean said no more and seemed to drift off into reverie.

After a while of just "sittin' and sippin'," Doc broke the silence and whispered, "Tell me, Mac, how is it with Kathleen?"

"Oh grand, you know. Things about the same, you know."

"I do know, Mac, and I know it's not our way to complain. And as long as that dear lady breathes a breath, she will be grand, even though that dread disease has cut her off from you and all she loves."

"Doc, is that really true? Sometimes I think she knows. Sometimes I think something seeps through to her, but then again I don't know. I have a sleepy eye, you know. It's very strange. If I close my very good right eye, and look with my bad eye, it's like—well, it's like I can see and I can't see. It's like lookin' through a wall. The wall is there and yet I can see something. Sometimes I hope its that way with that damnable Alzheimer's. There is a wall there, but maybe something in her sees through it, recognizes something, but there's no way of knowin', is there?"

"I guess not, Mac."

"Doc, if only there was some little sign, some hint that there's some spark hidin' there, it would do me a lot of good. You know she doesn't know me at all, as far as I can tell. Passin' by her is like walkin' through the hedgerows. You think there might be somethin' on the other side, but you don't know because there's a wall and a hedge between.

After some more banter about Sunday's hurling match, Sean drained the last drops from the pint and said, "Well, Doc, my hour here is just about up."

"Sure'n it is. You know when Father Dan was up there in the pulpit last Sunday recruitin' for a holy hour, I thought to myself, 'Well, Father, Sean and I have a holy hour, every night when he lets go of the care-takin' for just one hour and sits down here at Vaughan's with me.' "

"Ah, and sure it is, Michael—a holy hour it is. Well now, I'll be after headin' up the road to home."

"And I'll be walkin' with you, Sean."

As the two walked up the main street of Clifden, lights shone out from a few pubs and looking in they could see good folks enjoying a little *craic (pronounce: crack)* and a little more of Guinness—windows looking in—just what Sean did not have for Kathleen. When they came to the west end of town where the Sky Road forks up the hill to the right and Beach Road forks left down toward the bay, Doc waved goodbye and walked up the hill. Sean started down the road walking by Abbey Glen. As he neared the bottom of the hill, in the darkness, Sean thought he glimpsed a figure at the water's edge. Sure enough, there was someone down there and now he could hear a faint whimpering.

"Hello down there!"

At the sound of his voice, the figure at the water's edge turned and had in his hands a paper box. As Sean approached, he could tell that the weak whimpers were coming out of that box.

"Sean, it's me, Eddie McCoy."

"Well, Eddie, what would you be doing down here at this hour?"

"Well, you know that mutt of ours just had a litter. Five of the pups we gave out and the strongest male we kept. But that left us with this female runt of the litter. And you know how the wee children are; they wanted to keep it too. So this runt is going to disappear while they are sleeping, and they'll never know. I just walked down here to drown it."

"Drown it, you say? Let me take a look."

When Sean looked down into the box all he could see was two little eyes, a ball of fur, and from this tiny tot, not even a strong bark, just a whimper. Then Eddie lifted her out of the box by the scruff of her neck, and her head drooped down looking at the water. Then she gave a soft moan like the beginning of the keening at a wake. "Wait a minute, Eddie, you know our old dog Tatters gave up the ghost last year. Maybe I should take her. It might be grand havin' a tail waggin' a welcome at the door, especially since . . ." and his voice trailed off.

"Are ya sure, Sean? She's just a runt."

"Well, maybe a runt will do."

So the deal was struck. Out of the box she came. Eddie wrapped her in some newspaper like a fish and into Sean's coat pocket she went. Just her nose and beady eyes peaked out from this new world. And her body felt more warmth than since she first came out of her mother and had to struggle so hard just to find a friendly teat. After a while up the road, she stopped her whimpering and rustling around in the newspaper and got used to the bumpy ride.

The moon broke through scattered clouds and Sean could see their cottage up on the hill. The thatched roof shimmered in the moonlight and a thin wisp of peat smoke curled out of the chimney. A mellow glow illumined the front window and Sean could see the silhouette of Fiona sitting by the fire. What a dear aunt she was to take her turn each night watching Kathleen when Sean went for his "holy hour" at Vaughan's Pub.

As he made the turn up the lane, he said, "Well, pup, *Céad míle fáilte! (pronounce: kade meel-eh fawl-tche)* Well, maybe not a hundred thousand welcomes—maybe just two—one from me and one from Fiona. And what might we be calling you? Maybe 'Ship-wreck?' You sure were rescued from the sea! Or how about 'Jonah'—rescued from the whale? Naw, that wouldn't do, you're just a little wisp of a girl.

"All right, how about instead of 'Jonah'—'Joanie'?"

As he looked down, the two little eyes looked up at him quizzically and there was just a wee midget of a bark.

"Well, you can bark, can you? But not much, you won't be wakin' anybody up soon, will you?"

As he crossed the threshold, Fiona stood up with her knitting in hand and greeted him, "Well, bless the man of the house!"

"And bless you too! And how has Kate been doin' tonight?" With that, he glanced over to the corner where Kathleen sat in a chair dressed in her nightdress and robe. Through her fingers she kept fiddling with a strand of yarn. She gave no notice to his arrival.

"Well, she hasn't been walking so much tonight, Sean; she's just been sitting there for quite a while so I think she's ready to be put to bed. And, say now, what is that tryin' to crawl out of your pocket?"

"Oh, this one? Sure it's Joanie; I just rescued her from drowning down by the shore."

"Did you now? Well, let's have a look at her now!'

When Sean lifted her out of his pocket he got his first look at her. She was mostly black, with some white underbelly and a tiny white spot between her eyes. Her two little ears flopped down.

"Ah, let me hold her, Sean, the poor little thing looks terrified." When Fiona took her, her little paws clung to her blouse. "There, there, little one. It's a fine home you'll be havin' here!"

After rocking the little pup back and forth, Fiona looked at Sean and said, "I wonder if this little one would take to Kathleen?"

So she walked across the room and carefully placed the pup in Kathleen's lap. The little one looked up toward Kate's vacant stare, and worn out from her ordeal, snuggled up in her lap, wound her head around—with her nose toward her tail—and closed her eyes.

"If Kate only knew," Sean sighed.

And then as the peat fire's glow danced an aura around the immobile Kate, her withered hand let go of the yarn. It slowly moved across her lap and touched the pup. For a while it just lay there. And then ever so slowly, it began to stroke the pup, back and forth as if they had been friends forever. No words, no acknowledgment—just the petting.

And Sean stood still beneath Saint Brigid's cross on the mantle. He looked at Fiona and she looked back and this time it was their turn to be utterly still.

The Journey

In my travels through Ireland from Cork in the south to Donegal in the north and from Dingle in the west to Wicklow in the east— the meadows spoke to me and the birds and the animals and sea creatures spoke to me too. And as I observed the Irish, I came to agree with what Fiona had said in Dublin—oh yes, the ancient Celtic Spirit is in the very bones, if not in the immediate consciousness, of all the Irish generations.

Following Fiona's advice, I traveled to beautiful Dingle in Kerry where the green earth rolls down to the sand. Thunder drums roll through the valleys. And the wind rises and falls, rippling the sea. I came there to the Dingle harbor to seek a sea creature of mythic stature. Ancient Celtic lore believed in merrows—sea creatures seemingly half woman and half seal capable of living on land as well as sea. William Butler Yeats testified that these half sea creatures sometimes married men and one was known to live in Bantry! They have been brought to our attention lately by the movie *The Secret of Roan Inish*—the "secret" being the existence of a merrow, half woman and half seal.

"Fungie"

Fungie of Dingle is no merrow but he has grown to mythic fame. For Fungie's interaction with humans has been merrowlike. Fungie is the well-remembered dolphin of Dingle Bay who liked nothing better than to play and cavort with humans. Perhaps Fungie is a widower. He has no mate. Without kith or kin or the companionship of other dolphins, Fungie has adopted the boaters and fishermen of Dingle as his family and as of this writing they have honored the friendly dolphin as their own kin for some fourteen years.

Fungie became the subject of a film, *The Dolphin's Touch*, made in 1988 by Dr. Horace Dobbs. From that moment, Fungie became an international star. When I went to Dingle Harbor and paid ten pounds to take the boat out to see Fungie, I was told, "Your full money back if you do not encounter Fungie."

I asked, "Have you ever had to make a refund?"

"Never!" came the reply.

So we sailed out toward the ocean. The view was majestic, Mount Brandon brooding on the horizon and great slate cliffs dropping down to the sea on either side like two bookends with coves. On the shore, hedgerows like jumbled rosaries spread out into a pattern of pastures.

Sure enough, before we could reach the open sea, Fungie came right up to us and then did some twists and leaps and turns just to entertain us and himself. Sometimes Fungie swims with humans. At other times, he might decide just to jump right over a small boat! Dr. Horace Dobbs the filmmaker believes that dolphins are therapeutic for humans. Observing them summons up some deep instinct in the human to leap up out of whatever holds us down, whether it might be worry or even something more heavy like depression. The fact is that people of all ages do come to have their hearts gladdened by the leaping dolphin.

Perhaps Fungie is a trendsetter. More and more animals are being brought to hospitals and to care centers as important visitors for the sick. Their presence tends to lift spirits and calm anxiety. In Florida, Dr. David Nathanson would love to have Fungie, for he has pioneered "dolphin therapy"—children's interaction with a dolphin and immersion in warm water! The goal of dolphin-human therapies is to bring about small victories for children with brain damage, autism, cerebral palsy, and other neurological disorders.

"Falling for a Dolphin"

Playwright Heathcoate Williams came to Dingle, met Fungie, and wrote "Falling for a Dolphin." His words come close to expressing the ancient Celtic kinship with animals, birds, and sea creatures. When he observed Fungie's great eyes peering at him, he described the effect on himself of having his mind recharged and the kinship he experienced as "two minds blending—your mind reaching out and becoming one with another."

This intuitive feeling exemplifies in some ways the ancient Irish interaction with other creatures, not seeing them as foreign objects but rather experiencing them in an I–Thou relationship. They were accepted as fellow travelers and relatives on land and sea. It is significant that Ireland completely surrounded by ocean waters does not exploit the great creatures of the sea. Neither dolphins nor whales can be hunted within its territorial waters.

The Shepherd in the Hills

After Dingle, I journeyed on to the Ring of Kerry, to a carpeted green hillside, where I watched a modern young shepherd working his flock with two bright-eyed and totally dedicated sheep dogs. Black on top, with white underbellies, and white tipped feet, they were like runners tensed at their starting blocks. Their eyes were riveted on the shepherd. They could not wait to get started. When he blew a certain note on his whistle, off they went. They shot up the hillside like two demons. When they reached their goal—a small flock of sheep—they positioned themselves one on each side. And then they sat down, just watching. Then the shepherd blew a different note and they began to herd the sheep down the hill. As the shepherd would blow certain notes on his whistle, the dogs would react with different moves until they finally delivered the sheep right to the shepherd's feet. And then they sat, their tongues hanging out, very pleased with themselves as well they should be. The whole graceful operation was like a choreographed performance. They and the shepherd were in a deep sense one. Their ears were his hands just as surely as if he had climbed the hill and ushered the sheep down himself. Kinship? Oh yes! Here were three spirits, human and animal, in perfect concert together.

Good Shepherd or Good Sheep Dog?

The gospels tell us Jesus is like a good shepherd. Perhaps Jesus is also like a good sheep dog—alert, vigilant, and anxious for the safety of the sheep. The poet Francis Thompson thought so. He called Jesus "the Hound of Heaven," a hound dog who pursues us down the nights and down the days.

Another Ancient Shepherd

Watching the sheep dogs work reminded me of another shepherd of olden days. He was a teenager—only sixteen—when he kept a lonely vigil with his sheep on the mountains of Antrim. Did he have a sheep dog to help him? Possibly. But in his solitude, he had neither books nor other humans for solace. Baptized as a youth, he had not been a fervent Christian. In fact, in his own confession he identified himself as "unlearned" and "not knowing the true God," even though his father was a deacon and his grandfather a priest! (He sounds not too different from some of the modern youth on Grafton Street whose seeming lack of faith was lamented by Michael in the coffeehouse!)

And now as a kidnapped slave in Ireland, he was certainly cut off from Sunday worship or any church rituals. So what nourished him spiritually? There was nothing there but the sun, the stars, the sheep and other wild creatures he encountered as he kept watch. The only scripture he possessed was in his memory. So Padraic spent his nights and days outside in the great cathedral that had the sun and the stars for its ceiling. His carpet was the green grass. His only companions were the bounding deer, skipping rabbits, and the grazing sheep. And there on the mountains, Jesus, the Hound of Heaven—like a good sheep dog—relentlessly pursued the young Padraic. And Patrick tells us, "The Lord opened the understanding of my unbelieving heart that I might recall my sins and turn with all my heart to the Lord my God."

The Hound of Heaven

After his escape from Ireland the "Hound of Heaven" chased Saint Patrick back to Erin. And as myth would have it, his kinship with animals served him well. The ancient myths surrounding Patrick tell us the story of him and his monks being pursued by hostile troops of King Loegaire. To elude this pursuit Patrick and his retinue "shapeshifted" into a herd of deer and bounded away from the enemies' pursuit! Out of this story came the beautiful prayer of Patrick—the Breastplate, or Lorica. This story links the early Irish saints and the ancient Celtic kinship with animals, birds, and sea creatures and the whole natural world. This kinship with nature permeated his prayer:

I arise today
Through the strength of heaven:
Light of sun,
Radiance of moon,
Splendor of fire,
Speed of lightning,
Swiftness of wind,
Depth of sea,
Stability of earth,
Firmness of rock.
Saint Patrick's Breastplate

Shapeshifting

Caitlin Matthews, a renowned student of ancient Celtic lore, tells us that finding and working with an animal helper is a prerequisite for ancient shamans throughout the world. We can infer from this that the animal helpers possess an ancient wisdom of their own that can be of help to the seeker of wisdom. Both modern biology and cosmology and our present knowledge of the evolutionary process would validate that there is a mysterious ancient wisdom possessed by our animal ancestors.

It is estimated by cosmologists that vertebrate animals appeared 510 million years ago; jawed fish, 425 million years ago; dinosaurs, 235 million years ago; birds, 150 million years ago; whales and horses, 55 million years ago; cats and dogs, 35 million years ago; etc.—all of these predated human presence by eons. These creatures have known and adapted to the earth long before any humankind appeared. Do they possess their own wisdom as a result of this long process? The shamans thought so and they believed they could have access into the animal world through some kind of transmigration or shapeshifting—the human soul being sent into another form, as Patrick was shapeshifted into a deer!

Ancient Wisdom

The salmon is one example of a wisdom creature for the Celts. There was a mythic "salmon of knowledge" that swam in the river Boyne. It was believed that the first person to catch it and eat it would possess deep knowledge and wisdom. The Christian Celts would eventually call the Christian act of faith, the "salmon's leap"!

Recent research has examined the almost magic way that salmon and other creatures migrate over vast distances. Some scientists today are coming to believe that migrating creatures use the magnetic fields of the earth. Thus migrating fish and birds can ascertain how far north or south they are by sensing and reading the earth's magnetic fields! This is a process that no human yet has learned.

Animal Kinship and the Celtic Saints

When I traveled on to Donegal, I walked in the footsteps of the great Saint Colmcille whose nickname was "Columba—The Dove." There is a folktale about him that has survived the ages. Colmcille exiled himself to the island of Iona because of a battle that he promoted that resulted in many deaths. On Iona, he was attempting to build a monastery. However every night what had been built in the day was thrown down. He was puzzled by this and sought a solution. One day he sighted a half-woman, half-fish at the shore. So he sought her counsel and she gave it and the problem was solved. There are many layers to this story, not the least of which is the holy saint taking counsel from a wise woman and from another species. (In the Hebrew Book of Proverbs, Wisdom is personified as a woman.)

Colmcille's love for animals is renowned. There is also a tale about Colmcille giving shelter and refuge to a wounded crane. He gave instructions to a monk to watch for a weary and wounded crane that would arrive from Ireland. The crane was to be afforded three days of rest and generous hospitality from the monks. Then Colmcille said the crane could return to the "sweet region of Ireland." Perhaps in this, there is a longing to return also to Ireland from his own exile on the island of Iona.

Katherine Scherman, in her book *The Flowering of Ireland,* relates the story that as death draws near for Colmcille, a faithful white horse comes and lays his head against Colmcille's breast and weeps. When another monk tries to drive the horse away, Colmcille stops him and tells the monk, in effect, that God himself has revealed to the horse that Colmcille would soon die. So he blessed the horse as it turned sadly to leave him.

Columbanus

The stories of the early Irish saints are filled with incidents where they interact with other creatures and these interactions bring knowledge or healing experiences. Another remarkable Irish saint of the sixth century—Columbanus—followed the path of adventure for Christ and took the brightness of the gospel back into a Europe where it had grown dim. After establishing many other monastic settlements, he laid his last foundation at Bobbio in the north of modern Italy. We are told that when he needed solace and comfort, he went into the woods and communicated with the animals and birds. The exploits of Columbanus lived on in Bobbio, and his Celtic spirituality of kinship with animals and birds may have remained in that area and later times influenced Saint Francis of Assisi in developing such a kinship.

Why We Need the Third Secret?

So I would suggest the third secret of the Celtic Spirit is kinship with the natural world, especially close relationships with animals, birds, and sea creatures. Why do we need to rediscover this secret for our own time, culture, and place? Wendell Berry, in his book *The Unsettling of America, Culture and Agriculture*, suggests an answer by telling us that our modern culture has begun to see the whole creation as simply raw material to be transformed by machines into a manufactured paradise and thus our modern world would respect creation only insofar as it could be used by humans. Seeing the whole creation as raw material to be used in any "efficient" manner that satisfies our immediate personal needs is an attitude that engulfs us all. When we take a young calf away from its mother, enclose it in a box from which it cannot move in any direction, fill it with antibiotics, and deliberately make it anemic so that it will appear as white meat on the plate of some connoisseur of veal, we treat this creature simply as raw material. This is a prime example of a loss of kinship with the animal world. Not only does it degrade the calf, it dehumanizes the human "gourmet" for it removes the soulfulness from the creatures all around us. There must be a better middle way between this kind of disrespect and the other extreme of giving "sacred cows" precedence over humans. Saint Thomas Aquinas finds this middle way by indicating that there are differing degrees of soulfulness in the order of creation, each deserving a measure of respect. The American Indians understood this by killing only the buffalo they really needed and giving thanks to the buffalo for the giving up of his life so that humans might live. Today in Ireland, with some exceptions, for the most part, animals are treated with care and raised in rural settings that respect their dignity.

There are several other reasons we need to rediscover the secret of animal kinship with humans. We need to be inspired by their grace and beauty, learn from them our place in the order of creation, be humbled by their unique contributions, be encouraged by their transformations, and be companioned by domestic animals' unconditional love.

Grace and Beauty

Travel over the back roads and lanes of Galway and you will see, between the beautiful stones piled upon stones, pastures and corrals inhabited by beautiful horses. Often in the spring, frisky colts gambol round their mothers. The Irish have an ancient love affair with their horses, whether it is the Connemara ponies or the sleek race horses. The ancient pre-Christian myth of Cuchulainn describes the joy of glimpsing horses moving on the plain like a mountain mist: "The fast step—the joyful step of the horses coming towards us."

For the "joyful step" of the Irish horses today, go to the Punchestown horse racing festival in Kildare. Observe the race horses thundering over a grass course and then leaping over the famous "big double," jumping onto a bank and then off it again. Observe the spindly legs that are able to carry their enormous weight at breakneck speed—up, over, and beyond. And catch the expressions of admiration and love in the faces of the racing crowd that are well versed in the exploits of great horses. As the panting horses strain toward the finish line, they in some way carry with them the human hopes of being winners and snatching victory against all the odds.

Whether it is the winning horse breaking the finish line, or the brave salmon leaping up a waterfall, these other creatures offer us inspiration and courage to win our own races or leap over great obstacles. They also enliven us with powerful images of grace and beauty.

On the Road—The Farmer and His Cows

Part of the mystique of Ireland is driving along a country road and coming upon a farmer just ahead driving his cows home for the milking, or standing on a road in Donegal and seeing the sheep gazing far above on the mountainside, like white dots on a green carpet. Or sometimes they can be found munching nonchalantly by the side of the road. They give you a puzzled look that says, "What are you doing on our road?" In these scenes, the farmer, the cows, the sheep all blend into a panorama of ecological compatibility.

Irish Ecological Consciousness

The ecological balance of the human with other creatures is attested by many Irish writers. Amy Sher has called the Irish short story writer Liam O'Flaherty, who grew up in the Aran Islands in the

twentieth century, one of the first "preachers" of ecological consciousness. In his short story, "The Old Woman," O'Flaherty offers an
Irish vision of the dignity of all creatures within God's purpose:

> "What horrid things there are in God's world."
> "Don't say that, Julia," the old woman said.
> "There are only lovely things in God's world.
> Everything that God made has a divine purpose."

Soulfulness

Within this century we may reach a point where we will build
mighty domes on bleak Mars. Within these domes there will be
every sort of human convenience and technological wizardry. Will
this artificial "world" have a soulfulness? Or will it provide a
"scarred and blighted" human existence? We humans need the
precious soulfulness of animals, tame and wild. Their beauty and
gracefulness reveals to us a unique glory that lifts our soul. Even
in the midst of busy cities I have encountered raccoons, coyotes,
possums, even foxes. An encounter with a wild creature is a special
moment. It stirs something very deep in the human psyche. Without
them, and the eradication of other species, our world is diminished.
And without them, we lose our moorings in creation, for the creator
has established an arrangement or order of life and we need
animals on one side just as we need angels on the other. For we
share our reason with the angels and our bodies with the animals.

The Wild

But what of the "bloody law of tooth and fang" which we find in
the wild animal world? What are we to learn from that? Perhaps
we need to be reminded that no matter how peaceful we think we
are, we too in the darkness of our human shadows possess that
same savage animal tendency. And we need not to ignore its
potency but to tame its excesses.

Wildness—"The Preservation of the World"

Beyond that need, Thoreau in his essay on walking made the
rather astounding statement that "In wildness is the preservation

of the world." In his prophetic ecological book, *The Great Work*, Thomas Berry follows up on this by stating that it is wildness "that has gifted us with our instinctive drives toward finding food and shelter and protecting the young. It is our innate wildness that triggers us living creatures 'to sing and dance, and fly through the air and swim through the depths of the sea.'"

But if we were to tame all the wildness, eliminate the wild species, and subdue all the wilderness, a great barrenness would replace a well-spring of energy. Robert Bly has also written about the necessity of the human male retaining some of the "wild man's tendencies." (The pre-Christian Celts were indeed wild men. When the Romans faced their naked bodies painted for battle, they said, "We will go no farther" and instead built Hadrian's wall to seal them from the wild men beyond.)

Wild Energies

The Christian Celts tamed the extremes of Celtic wildness by their asceticism but retained the wild energies of moving fearlessly beyond the margins of the safe and the predictable. A lesson from the Celtic Spirit might be that we need both the wild and civilization, not either/or.

Domestic Animals

No wonder the animals were companions of the Celtic saints. They were part of the warp and woof of their spirituality as well. Those ancient Christian Celts grasped in their minds and spirits that other creatures are worthy of companionship and sometimes even of emulation. In an ancient century an Irish scribe writing in his cold monastery cell looked up from his parchment and had his spirit warmed by Pangor Ban, his friend the cat. The scribe remains unknown but the cat became renowned!

> My friend Pangor Ban and I
> engage our own pursuits.
> His delight is hunting mice,
> Mine is writing truths.

Irish literature is often friendly toward the fellow creatures of other species who accompany us on our journeys. The Irish short story writer Frank O'Connor wrote a story called "Requiem," In this story an old woman comes to the parish priest to have a Mass said for "Timmie." Only after a long conversation does the priest discover that Timmie is her deceased poodle. He then tells her it is impossible to say a Mass for a dog. In her response, the old woman goes beyond Saint Thomas Aquinas' definition of soulfulness possessed by animals:

> "I'm as good a Catholic as the next, but I'd say it to the Pope himself . . . They *have* souls . . . Anything that can love has a soul. Show me that bad woman that thanked God her husband was dead and I'll show you someone that maybe hasn't a soul, but don't tell me that my Timmie hadn't one. And I know as I'm standing here that somewhere or other I'll see him again." [1]

Dogs, from the red-sheened Irish setters to the Irish wolf-hounds, as well as ordinary hounds of farm and hearth, are numerous on the Irish scene. And who has not met someone who has experienced the unconditional love of such an animal and who possessed an innate hope that the creature would be present in an afterlife?

There is an Irish pub story perhaps based on Frank O'Connor's "Requiem" where an Irishman comes in to see the priest and requests a memorial Mass for his dog Blackie. When the priest refuses, he begins to walk out, murmuring, "Well, I guess I'll have to take the $10,000 stipend I was going to give you and try the Presbyterian Church down the street."

Immediately the priest cries out, "Oh, wait a minute. You didn't mention to me whether your dog was a Catholic dog. If that's the case, a Presbyterian Church would not do and your memorial Mass would only be proper here!"

Our Postmodern Experience

But what of us who traverse the busy freeways where there are no ambling milk cows, or who live far from the sea. In our post-modern culture where can we catch the Celtic Spirit of kinship and learn lessons from other creatures? Being a keen observer is a start. On the back deck of a home in the heart of the city, friends

Ron and Joann and I watched a robin's nest tucked into the eaves of the house. We watched her as she fed her three babies and also as she painstakingly cleaned up their droppings with her beak and carried them out to be deposited away from the nest. "Don't foul your own nest!" is an ancient teaching from such a bird that remains quite current even for humans.

For those fortunate to live under a North American flyway, each spring and fall the migrating geese write lessons in the sky. They take turns breaking the path for each other. And if one should be downed by a hunter, two will peel off and land near the fallen comrade to accompany the victim in its dying or in its rising. As one poet once wrote: "We are all wayfarers and we have too little time to gladden the path of those who are on the way with us." The flying geese take the time. We might do as well. And although the scripture images the Holy Spirit as a dove, the Celts preferred the wild goose as their image of the Spirit!

Little children love to go to zoos. Watch them there. They have a delightful kinship with the other creatures. Perhaps in relationships with the animal world, we too might profit greatly by becoming "like little children." Kinship ultimately is an attitude. We can develop it or deplete it. It all depends on "how we see things" or other creatures who are our relatives.

Rather than experiencing a sense of oneness with other creatures all around, postmodern "humanity" becomes the "spoiled only child" on the earth. We have no animal brothers or sisters. We fail to notice or value the other creatures who walk, run, see, and share the earth with us unless we can use them for fuel, tools, or toys. We are like some child in a playpen enchanted only by toys we can manipulate. Such a playpen is ultimately a lonely island.

Seemingly, the postmodern worldview would have us stand alone and lonely, disconnected from any earth community. We cage the animals, pave over the meadows, sprawl over the greenery, and when we are finished, we are farther from one another than ever before. Paradoxically, when we learn of the early Celtic saints seeking remote places of solitude it seems mystifying to us that such a lively and socially oriented people could become so isolated. But were they? Walk through the lovely glen of Glendalough where Saint Kevin walked and talked with the raven and discover that he had companions all around—the birds of the sky and creatures of the field. And like all the Celts he communed with them. We need to discover the third of the Celtic secrets for our own lives. The Celtic worldview possessed coherence. The ancient Celts were one with all creatures, with all the vegetation, the earth itself, and the spirits just beyond. To be "one with" creation showers us with many blessings. An unfettered "divide, conquer, and develop attitude" toward the natural world results in a constant process of diminishment.

Celtic kinship with creation is much more than a fuzzy Disney-like, feel good attitude toward the animal world. The interaction of the Celtic saints with the natural world suggests a profound truth. For those Celts the Holy and the Sacred is present all around the circle of creatures and in the close-at-hand circle of spirits who spiral and weave through all of life. The great secret the ancient Celts reveal for us is that all are mystically one and one is mystically all!

Prayer

O God of all creation,
may I leap with the dolphin into joy.
May I vault with the horse over great obstacles.
And in the midst of hyper pace may I pause and amble
so that I begin to observe
the mystery of life all around me.

Journal Option:
The other creatures like the . . . teach me . . .

Notes: [1] "Requiem," in *Stories by Frank O'Connor: A Set of Variations*, Alfred A. Knopf, New York, NY, 1969, p. 313

CHAPTER FOUR

Enchantment
and
Allurement

The Fourth Secret
of the Celtic Spirit

Who is God,
and where is God,
of whom is God,
and where is his dwelling?

Has he sons and daughters,
gold and silver,
this God of yours?

Is he ever living?
Is he beautiful,
was his Son
fostered by many?

Are his daughters
dear and beautiful
to the men of the world?

Is he in heaven,
or on the earth?
In the sea,
in the rivers,
in the mountains,
in the valleys?

Speak to us
tidings of him:
How will he be seen,
how is he loved,
how is he found?

Is it in youth
or is it in old age
he is found?

These are the questions asked of Saint Patrick by two lovely maidens at the Well of Clibach. How Patrick came to meet these maidens in Eire—therein lies a marvelous story. And it is a tale of adventure and enchantment. As we have seen, the saga of Saint Patrick is an epic tale of being kidnapped and exiled but later being drawn back to the people who enslaved him. This is the story of how he would return again to Erin to walk a blessing path and baptize in the sacred waters of the holy well of Clibach. Patrick returned because the land and its people allured and enchanted him in his dreams. And therein lies the fourth secret of the Celtic Spirit: enchantment and allurement.

However, this fourth secret of the beauty of enchantment preceded Saint Patrick in the Druid groves. And it lived on long after Patrick. For from then on it was a vital part of the great "Jesus story." It was this enchanting and adventurous story that appealed to the Druids and the Irish chiefs. And it was the hero savior that allured the daughters of Erin.

The telling of the Jesus story to the pagan Celts was so appealing that the old Druid gates were opened and Jesus was welcomed in. This marked a crossing of boundaries from the Druid days to the new era of the Christian Irish-Celts.

So it was at this time, between the twilight of the Druids and the rising of the Christ light, that Saint Patrick met these two lovely daughters of a pagan Irish king at the holy well of Clibach. It was with wide-eyed wonder that the two young women questioned Patrick about the new God he proposed to them.

These two seekers of wisdom were already aware of allurement and wonder through their old religion. So they asked if Patrick's God could allure them as well. And then Patrick gave them his wondrous response:

> Our God is the God of all things.
> The God of heaven and earth,
> The God of the sea and the streams,
> The God of the sun, moon, and stars,
> The God of the great high mountains and the deep glens,

The God above heaven, in heaven, and under heaven.
And he has a household—heaven and earth,
And the sea and all that they contain.

Our God is a God of allurement and enchantment—this is the message of Patrick for the two lovely girls mentored by the Druids who were well trained to know enchantment and beauty when they saw it. For these girls their conversation with Patrick would mean a crossing over of the boundary between the old Druid way and the new Christ way.

A Story from the Celtic Twilight

Here is a mythic story about such a "crossing over boundaries time," as a traditional Irish storyteller might imagine, embellish, and tell it.

Once upon another day, in that same betwixt and between time, when the Druids still had some sway but when Patrick and Brigid had poured new wine into new wineskins, there lived a boy named Liam and this is Liam's story of enchantment:

"When I was twelve, I was fostered out to the family of an Irish chief who lived on the banks of Lough Ree. This chieftain had two foster daughters, Eithne, who was sixteen years old and fair, and Marga, who was thirteen and a budding rose. They both were strong of heart and supple of limb like their mother, Derva. At first Marga and I played together like a brother and sister, like two dearest friends. But in the next spring, a wondrous thing began to happen. Marga's breasts began to rise like the paps of Enu, and the sun shone more brightly on her hair and there was no more of climbing trees or scaling rocky cliffs. In some strange way, she began to move away from me while at the same time my heart began to move toward her.

And then a day came when a chariot arrived with her father at the reins and she rode away to I knew not where. The very next day, my foster sire looked at a tree and announced it to be flawed and that it must be trimmed or pruned. I knew the flaw and my cheeks reddened for I had carved her name, "Marga," upon its upper trunk. So I spoke out immediately and announced: "Let me tend it, Sire; I shall climb it and mend its flaw."

"So be it!" announced my foster sire.

When he left, I climbed the tree and carved away the name of Marga, and covered it over with a brown paste so that no one would know my secret love.

That very night, I was awakened from sleep when I heard a commotion outside my window. When I looked out I observed a frightening sight, a troop of the little people the fairies, dancing round and round the hawthorne tree and they sang a song:

Around and around, three times around,
This tree defaced shall not remain.
Around, around, three times around,
Fall, Hawthorne Tree, fall to the ground!

And fall it did! And then the wee people grumped and chattered and dragged the felled tree into a hole in the ground and when they had descended into their world, they pulled a clump of earth to seal their passage into the deep. I crept back into the straw of my bed and pulled the sheepskin covers over me as though they could obscure the sight I had surely seen.

In the morning, the cutting of the tree disturbed the master of the house and I was much afraid of enduring his wrath. However, he was leaving in his chariot for a war council and he told his wife, Derva, to see to the matter. She was kindly and wise and she said to me: "My dear fosterling, perhaps the time has come for you to fly from this nest and seek your dreams. Pray tell, it would be better for you to leave before the king returns.

"One last word before your journey, turn your mind to Lugh, the great God of the Sun, and entrust to him your dream and then make your way on the road."

So the next morning at dawn, that in-between time, I greeted the sun and announced in my heart: "Great God of the Sun, my heart yearns for the enchantment I felt when I discovered the budding beauty of Marga, and may my quest bring me to Marga's gate."

And with that I set forth toward the sun rising in the east. It was a long journey to the east and I encountered many obstacles. Once, a herd of swine crossed the path and a boar took note of me and charged with great fury. It took all the might of my staff to repel him and send him squealing. There were also other creatures who befriended me and often a herd of gentle-eyed deer would lead me to life-giving water and ravens to delicious berries.

Ever eastward I went till I reached the great forest of Wicklow. The traipsing grew more difficult as I moved up and over hills and through valleys, sometimes having to make the salmon's leap across roaring torrents. Deeper and deeper I went and darker and darker the woods became.

Then one day in the depths of the forest, a white-robed figure loomed before me and asked, "What right do you have to traverse this sacred forest?"

"Only the right of a seeker of wisdom, sir." I answered.

"A seeker of wisdom, eh? What wisdom do you seek?"

"I seek the wisdom of enchantment. And I seek Marga who has laid her enchantment upon me."

"I know nothing of Marga but of enchantment I know the secrets, for I am a Druid. Do you not realize that you are in the midst of enchantment? The trees do sing and their branches dance in the arms of the winds! And the life source weaves and spirals its way through every glen. Do you not know that you shall not even begin to know your way till you are halfway through the forest? Do you not know that you are already one-third of your life's journey? And do you not know that you are at a boundary line, a thin place, a sacred transit and I stand here to guard it?"

"Kind sir, I bow in reverence to you and only ask that you might direct me toward enchantment and the thin transit that lies between me and the enchanting Marga."

"So, you are humble and willing to learn. Very well, I shall teach you, for our old ways are passing and I shall not have many to teach anymore. First, be attentive. Look about. Notice everything around you as you journey. If you do so, you will discover enchantment all around. As to your future journey, you will discover other beauties and your heart will be moved. Be steadfast and continue on. Move till you hear the roar of falling waters. There make the salmon's leap and follow your allurement to the sea, and then westward and around the tip of Eire where her peninsula fingers stretch out to the West, and someday you shall meet the wisdom that you seek. Now pass by."

And so I continued on through the forest, day by day, year by year, until one day I heard the roar of falling waters. I journeyed toward the sound and came to a glen and then beheld a wondrous sight. White crested waters leaped down over black rock, cascading, spinning, and splashing. And so I stood in silence, as the Druid told me to do, awed and humbled by the tumbling waters, which were framed by clusters of golden gorse. When I reached the waterfall, I stood still again.

After a long silence I heard a voice from the waters: "You may make the salmon's leap now, and then go southwestward on a tiring journey until you meet the roiling sea. Or you may walk around these rocks and venture into the hollow crevice between the rock wall and the plunging water. No need to tax yourself anymore. Take the easier way and stay with me. "The voice from behind the falling waters was sweet and the place to which she invited me easier to enter.

And then I remembered the Druid's challenge: "Make the salmon's leap and turn to the sea and go round the furthest tip of Eire and on to the north." So I ignored the siren voice and followed my own inner voice of allurement. I retreated and then summoning all my might and speed sprinted toward the stream that flowed away from the waterfall. With all my strength I leapt across.

The path now led toward the sea. I could smell its saltiness long before I could see it. Finally, that glorious day came when I stood upon a cliff and saw its waves crashing against the stones below. And now I could experience what only had been told to me before in the stories of seanachies—the allure of the mighty sea.

As I followed the path beside the sea for a long, long time, one twilight I came upon a pack of seals sunning themselves on the rocks below. And then a wondrous sight appeared, a woman of scarlet hair with the sun glinting through it, full bosomed, but a seal body below! So every eventide, I would come back to this spot, and every time move closer to this beautiful creature. And every time that I would move closer, my heart would beat stronger, for she was graceful and alluring.

After loving her from afar, the day came when she allowed me into her presence. Day after day, I grew closer to her. She was Acquainne and she laughed like the wind and swam like the graceful swan, and skimmed the waters like the swift salmon. Soon, my heart turned from fondness to passion. Then one starlit night we lay together and I became one with the very sea itself.

And the time passed and she brought forth a daughter, Deidre, and she too was fair of face but with the flippers of a seal! When I gazed upon the child's face, her smile enchanted me. And then she too grew in grace and ocean skills. Each eventide, I would swim with Acquainne and Deidre, sporting upon the breaking waves. And then one evening, the seal pack began to grunt and move about and push away from the rocky shore. I ran to the water's edge and there just above the waters were the faces of Deidre and Acquainne. They smiled smiles that warmed the frigid water.

"This is our transit time," said Acquainne. "You have tasted the wine of love and the salt of the sea. It is now time for us to go and for you to be on your way, for did not the Druid say, 'You must travel around the tip of Eire and north beyond and our journey is ever southward.' " And with that, these two most lovely creatures, one the very fruit of my loins, swam away, leaving me with tears more salty and sad than all the seas.

And so I journeyed on, more bent over than before. At eventide, I would pull down the black sky and its cold stars as a cloak and enter into the cave of my dreams. And so many of my dreams showed Deidre and Acquainne swimming away out of my sight and I would awake teary-eyed and sweating. After so many long and lonely nights, finally that day came when I reached the furthest tip of Eire and looked out upon the western sea.

That night, I had a dream different from all the rest. Marga appeared in a dream, no longer the child of my memories, but full grown and more beautiful than I could have ever imagined. When she spoke, her voice was soft and sweet and she whispered: "You are about to enter into the sacred and last third of your life. Travel northward and at a sacred well near the cliffs called Moher, you will meet a woman at the well drawing water. She is a mighty woman of great wisdom. She is a light bearer and she will tell you of your journey's fulfillment."

So I made the long trek northward until I came near the cliffs called Moher and then I walked into a glen and there she was, the stalwart woman, standing with two maidens and two young men with long hair in the back but shaved in front. As I approached, I could hear her lilting laughter. Upon her shoulders she wore an emerald wool cloak. Her milky cream face was sprinkled with a few freckles and she had mirthful and dancing eyes of green. With her sleeves rolled up she brought forth water from the well and filled the jars of her companions.

When she noticed me, she smiled a welcome that would warm the sun, and the two maidens and the two young men made a slight bow and departed, carrying the jars of water. "You come from afar, do you not?"

"Yes, I am Liam and have been on a long circle of a journey, from Lough Ree, through the Wicklow forest, around the tip of Eire, and here now to this place. And, good woman, who may I ask are you?"

"Some call me 'Mary of the Gael.' Some call me 'Lighter of the Fire and Keeper of the Hearth,' or even 'Bride,' but my given Christian name is Brigid and I serve that high King who has sent his lovely Son on the hero's quest. I wear his cross around my neck, for I am pledged to him and to his journey."

So I replied: "I do not know this king of yours and his hero son, but I was sent forth by Lugh, the God of the Sun, on my life's quest."

Brigid smiled a knowing smile and asked: "And what is your quest, Liam?"

"At an early age I was enchanted by the loveliest of maidens—Marga. And then, a sad day, she was taken away. When I set out on my quest, I asked Lugh to lead me to the enchantment I knew with Marga and someday lead me to her very portal."

Brigid replied, "Liam, I have traveled far and wide and now I pastor a double monastery of women and men so I have long experience in reading the hearts of men as well as women. I have become an *anam cara*—a "soul friend" to many. Do you desire such friendship?"

"I would be honored," I replied, "for I have traveled long and far on my circular journey and I am weary from the walking and my heart is heavily burdened. On this journey I have known hardship, but also allurement and passion. I have known the joy of love and the anguish of separation. If you can read the human heart, please read mine and tell me where enchantment lies."

"Liam, I am aware that you met one of the remaining Druids in the forest of Wicklow. He guarded a boundary line between the old Druid ways and the new ways of the hero Christ. He advised you well and when you moved beyond him, you began a journey out of the old ways. Your love for the merrow was the last encounter with the old ways of the fairies and merrows. Do not despise those ways, for in many ways they have served us well in helping us know that there is more to life than meets the eye. And so we do not dislodge them from their forts beneath the earth or the seas through which the merrows swim. We let them be.

"You knew love and birth with the merrow and all good love comes from God. But now our new God who is older and greater than any other gods—our God, who is one in three, reaches down his long arm and enters into our lives. Unbeknownst to you, when you made the salmon's leap, new spirits accompanied you. One was Michael the Archangel with the golden shield and he appointed another angel to always be at your side. And, as you journeyed on through the best of times and the worst of times, this guardian was beside you. As you know, in the old ways, Samrain was a thin time when the spirits of the other world came very close. The spirits that have allegiance to the new King and to the hero Son live beyond but they are still very close also. They are the saints and the angels and their home is to the west on the Isle of Saints. And they have brought you here to me."

"But what of my quest for enchantment and my desire to reach the portal of Marga?"

"Liam, do you not realize that when you carved her name upon the tree you also impressed her name upon your heart? And in searching for the enchanting Marga you have discovered enchantment all around. Marga has allured you and opened the gates of enchantment for you. She now walks with the angels and has been your gentle guide, your muse, your intercessor with the great King. And you have discovered enchantment all around, for Marga is the gentle hills. She is the sacred forest. She is the graceful waterfall. She is always the fragrant and alluring breeze of spring.

"Some time ago, unbeknownst to you, she departed for the Isle of Saints, but she has always been very close to you, for the saints and angels are always just one step away. You prayed that you might reach her portal and you have. Look to the setting sun. She is there on the Isle of Saints beyond the western rim, but she also is close to you in every flower and every breeze, for you see this world and the next mingle together. So long ago in your youth, you saw her as no one else could. You saw her with the eyes of first love, and ever after she has been the lens, allowing you to discover enchantment all around.

"You have made the great circle journey and have reached her portal. I must now be after returning to my monastery for the hour of Vespers. Will you accompany me?"

And so I did, walking eastward again, closing the circle. And when we reached the monastery walls, I saw a wondrous sight—a great stone high cross with a circle round its arms! And I said to Brigid, "Tell me more about the great hero and about his circle with the cross."

Brigid led me toward the door and said, "Indeed I will, *anam cara.*"

And I looked up to the sky, and the stars no longer seemed cold. Instead, they seemed to flicker and dance with great joy.

Our Enchanted Journeys

So is this story Liam's alone? I think not. Some of it is my story and some of it is yours. It is the story of anyone who has known first love. It is the story of that unique and enchanting moment when a parent looks into the face of a newborn. It is the story of passionate love and of unrequited love. It is the story of loss and separation. And for those who take the time to follow the Druid's urging—those who walk through life and take the time to see enchantment all around. Liam's story is my story. Liam's story is your story.

Enchantment

Anyone who has journeyed to Ireland and stood at the cliffs of Moher, or walked through the forests of Wicklow, or stood near the waterfall at Powers Court and have seen it gracefully draping down from the cliff top like a pure white bridal veil—has seen enchantment all around.

Today, I talked to Barbara, a Jungian therapist just returned from her fifth journey to Erin. And I asked her: "Did you find enchantment in Ireland? And if you did, what was it like?"

She paused, pondered, and then she said, "Oh yes! I found enchantment in the very landscape itself, with its ancient ruins and even when the mists swirl and the rain kisses the earth the land is beguiling. What was it like for me? It was like coming to a sacred place where somehow I had been before, a place of illumination, a place that fed my very soul. Enchantment? I guess to put it in one word—Charm! Maybe the Irish word, *Thar cinn!*—'Over the top!' That's it! It is charm over the top!"

Webster

Far better to ask a journeyer like Barbara than to consult *Webster's Dictionary*, for it is at a loss for words in trying to describe the word "enchantment." It says it means to "be enchanted!" which tells us nothing. So it should be, for enchantment is an experience beyond words. Webster does better is describing the word "enchant." It tells us that this word means to "delight to a high degree, to charm, to fascinate, to captivate." Yes! From such enchantment comes the allurement that draws journeyers to Ireland over and over!

Enchantment in Literature

Brian Swimme, one of my own mentors, in his marvelous book *The Universe Is a Green Dragon,* assures us that our destiny is enchantment! When we walk through a forest and out again we should bear the mystery of the forest with us. When we listen and notice we will discover the human and divine worlds flowing together. Even gravity is a form of allurement. Swimme reminds us that alluring activity permeates the universe and the universe itself is our best teacher in alluring love. The moving tides, the pale moonlight, the dancing mountains. ("Yes," says Swimme, the cosmologist, "the mountains do move!") They are to teach us about allurement and enchantment. When we learn to be one with the enchantment of creation we are initiated into the heart of the universe. Swimme affirms "if the initiation is long, and filled with doubt and suffering, the learning takes hold deeply."

And this is the path that Liam took. He did come out of the forest and began to be attentive. His initiation too was long and sometimes contained suffering, but he was never bored. Nor shall we be bored as we seek enchantment.

"Pay attention!" said the old Druid to Liam in the forest. James Joyce in *Ulysses* says the same. His character has fixated his stare on a label on a bottle. When someone starts to disturb Bloom, Mulligan intervenes: "Preserve a Druid silence. His soul is far away." Joyce then adds that any object intensely regarded can be a gate of access to the dwellings of the gods. Whether for the Druids or the twenty-first-century spiritual seeker, calming down, paying attention, is the first step of the way to contemplation or contemplative prayer.

William Butler Yeats

As James Joyce wrote the greatest novel of the last century, it was William Butler Yeats who set the bar high for all Irish poets. Some two hundred years before Yeat's birth, his ancestors came from England to Ireland and passed on their English blood and Anglo Irish heritage. Yet Yeats obtained a Celtic spirit almost by osmosis from the soil and paths of Sligo and the country people who dwelled there. And from this came his passion for reviving the ancient Celtic culture.

Yeats was a searcher for the enchantment of Celtic folklore. He was born in Sligo and in his youth on holiday he loved to wander through her hills and listen to the stories of the people. They were stories filled with fairy tales and wondrous adventures and spirits inhabiting "enchanted woods." One of his resources was Paddy Flynn, who Yeats discovered living alone in the village of Ballisodare. The first time Yeats saw him, Paddy was asleep under a hedge with a blissful smile on his countenance. Yeats plumbed the imaginations and the folklore of Paddy and many more that he interviewed along the way. The stories that were told to Yeats held within them a spirit of enchantment. In the book *Celtic Twilight,* Yeats writes about the enchanted woods:

> I believe that when I am in the mood that all nature is full of people whom we cannot see. . . . Even when I was a boy I could never walk in a wood without feeling that at any moment I might find before me somebody or something. I had long looked for without knowing what I looked for. . . . I will not of certainty believe that there is nothing in the sunset, where our forefathers imagined the dead following their shepherd the sun. [1]

In his later life, Yeats would expand his restless search for spirits beyond sight by delving into the occult and the bizarre.

However, in his youth when he roamed the Sligo hills he was closest to the people who imagined themselves closest to the fairies.

In many ways, the life journey of the great poet Yeats was similar to the mythic journey of Liam. Early in his life, on January 30, 1889, a vibrant woman came into his life who was—as Marga was for Liam—the epitome of a luminous woman. He saw her with a poet's eyes and was enchanted on the spot. He described her complexion being like sunlight falling on apple blossoms and her figure standing before him framed by a window like a bouquet of apple blossoms. Her name was Maud Gonne and she was ardent in her devotion of the cause of a free Ireland. Yeats would later propose to her and be rejected. Yet throughout his life she would be the lens through which he too would deepen his love for all things Celtic.

There would be other strong women in his life, like Lady Gregory, his patron, and other lovers and eventually his wife, but Maud Gonne would remain his muse, inspiration and his *anam cara*—his "soul friend."

Fairies and Leprechauns

Travel in Ireland today and there are still old-timers who will tell you stories about the wee people. The stories are charming, but do they believe them still? This remains a question. Here are some comments overheard in a pub: When asked if he believed in fairies, an old geezer with a wool cap pulled down over his forehead and a face tinted red from the wind, replied: "Indeed I don't believe! . . . But the little buggers seem to be everywhere!" Another patron, when asked if he believed in God, responded: "Not at all! Thanks be to God!"

The Fourth Secret of the Celtic Spirit

Why has enchantment and allurement become a secret hidden from our twenty-first-century experience? One reason is because we are captives of virtual reality—not the real world of the universe. Another is that we are too rushed to notice the real world of nature. Another is that we skim over only the surface of reality.

There is an underlying principle beneath all the Celtic stories, all the Celtic myths, the world of the leprechauns and the merrows. The fundamental principle is that there is more around us than meets the eye. The genius of Saints Patrick and Brigid was not to condemn the rich fairy world and rob the Irish of their imaginative world, but rather to affirm their deep belief in a world where there is more than meets the eye. They agreed with that and taught the Irish that they were indeed surrounded by creatures of another world, that they were very close and these otherworldly creatures were the saints and the angels.

We need to rediscover an attitude of enchantment for the world around us. We cannot be enchanted all the time; there are bills to pay, clothes to wash, errands to run, but we would do well to bring into our lives moments of enchantment. In his wonderful book *The Re-Enchantment of Everyday Life*, Thomas Moore proclaims that our very souls have an absolute and unforgiving need for regular excursions into enchantment. In our culture we need to rediscover enchantment, for there is more than meets the eye:

Look again!
Is it just another rainy day in Erin?
Or does the Holy Mountain
pull over her shoulder
a cloak of mist and rain,
then shrug it off
and bathe
her face in the sun?
May I look again!
There is more
than first meets the eye!

Prayer

May God's goodness be ours,
May the mantle of Brigid be ours,
And well, and seven times well, may we spend our lives.
May we be an isle in the sea,
May we be a hill on the shore,
May we be a star in the darkness,
May we be a staff to the weak;
May the love Christ Jesus gave, fill every heart for us;
And may the love Christ Jesus gave, fill us for every one.

Guimis: Ár n-Athair or in language of country

Journal Option:
The enchantment that nourishes my soul . . .

Notes: [1] William Butler Yeats, *The Celtic Twilight,* A Signet Classic, The New American Library of World Literature, 501 Madison Ave., New York, NY, in arrangement with the Macmillan Co., 1962, p. 75.

CHAPTER FIVE

Story and Good Humor

The Fifth Secret of the Celtic Spirit

Walking the Burren — The Great Stories

(The Burren is a unique series
of rock formations that run along
the West Coast of Ireland.)

On the Burren, clouds dart.
Shadow fingers
dip into crevices
and feel their way
through layers upon layers
of the pre-human story.
Piled up gray rocks
page upon page—the cosmic story.
Gasses fuming, forming, hardening,
allured by lady gravity,
cooled into earth's hard bone.
Eons before human eyes could see.
Here before our parents' coupling
and all the ones before.

Walk the road below
between countless gray rocks,
hand picked, piled up on either side.
One upon another, no mortar in between.
What are the stories of the rock pilers?
Hard times, calloused hands, deprivation?
Did they walk the famine walk
in this wild Burren wilderness?
Now only birdsong hints of freedom.
Wild roses clamber over rigid rocks
reaching out, hiding their thorns.
Petals red from bleeding hands?
Our human story lies deeply hidden
in vials of blood and strands of DNA.

The road between the countless rocks
curves away and then looming up ahead
appears a gray slit-eyed Norman castle!
How many knights rode up this road?
How much blood was spilled upon it?
Washed away by clouds' tears.
Upon the castle turrets, slit eyes of old —
blind now — spilling oil down
upon a road of sadness and misty vapors.

But now the sun skips out from broken clouds
reaching its long hand down to the vine.
Radiant rose recalls garlands and gaiety.
Lovers hand in hand upon this road,
wedding carriages festooned, rolling forth.
And mounted men rollicking and
singing of the foray and the hunt.
There is every story upon this road
winding through the human eons.
Road, you have borne them all.
Tell us the stories of the journeys,
of leprechauns and fairies,
of gallant knights and fair ladies,
of great saints and luminous scholars,
of scoundrels and heroines.
From your primeval archives
unroll the scrolls of ancient memories.
Tell us your stories! Tell us your stories!

My Story

D addy, tell me a story!"—words I spoke when I was three years old. I know the year exactly because at age four we moved from our original house to a new house. Therefore my age three and four memories are encoded in the images and recollections from the old house. At my age three, my little sister, Mary Rose, died and I was left an only child. We lived next to a wooded ravine that was a shaded place of mystery. I remember a steel sign in the shape of a policeman who stood at the entrance to the ravine warning drivers not to enter. In the mind of an imaginative child, who dwelt in that forbidden territory, dragons? Perhaps.

I also have vivid memories of those years of climbing up on my father's knee and begging him to "tell me a story." I think he made up some of the stories and they were marvelous because my imagination could play along with his. Other stories he gleaned from books. One story I remember him telling me was of the Trojan Horse. My father had only a high-school education but he knew Greek mythology and much more.

Another time he told me about the thunder overhead and that some thought this loud noise came from the "gods bowling in the sky." In telling me these stories he led me into the wonderful world of imagination. From my earliest years I also remember tagging along with my father and mother to the library and them bringing home many books to read. What children derive today from Harry Potter, I received from books, but also from my own father's storytelling. What a blessing to have a parent who would feed my sacred imagination.

Ireland, the Land of Stories

After having traveled many times to Ireland, I now understand where my father's storytelling came from—an oral tradition handed down from the ancestors. For Ireland is a magical land where imagination flourishes and there is a story just beyond the next turn, or the next draft of Guinness. Often the fruits of Gaelic storytelling are mirth and laughter. Sometimes even faith enrichment. The sharing of stories in the Irish tradition turned conversation into an art form and out of this seedbed have sprung the fabled short stories where Irish storytellers excel.

Like some sort of stream flowing out from a holy well, Irish storytelling passed down from generation to generation. During the terrible emigration years of the famine, it would seem that many of the immigrants wanted to forget that awful road they walked and some of the old stories dried up. Still, even in their new experiences in North America, echoes of the old stories lingered on. My great-grandfather immigrated to northwest Iowa farming country and lived in a little Irish colony named after County Clare in Ireland. And there were still echoes of the fairies and banshees lingering in Iowa. For the story was told that there was a certain hollow passed by a gravel road and when the priest on sick calls at night drove his horse past it on his way to bring the sacraments, the horse would rear and grow wild. And so the priest had to go and bless that place for there were spirits there adverse to his pastoral care.

Mimicking the Ancestors

When the Irish American novelist, Michaela Gilchrist, author of *The Good Journey,* was interviewed by Diane Hartman of the *Denver Post,* she revealed the origin of her own storytelling. Perhaps she also hinted about an ancient Celtic attitude regarding "original sin" that was more lighthearted than the Augustinian view. Her father was a hard-working teamster living on the "Irish Hill" in Omaha, the same Irish enclave where my own father was raised. Like my father did for me, Michaela's dad read stories to her constantly. In talking about her origins, she credits a loving family and the influence of all the generations on her growing up. And she illustrates that with a story:

> In the second grade you have to make your second confession. All the girls were kneeling in a row. Now I was considered the smart, homely one. I remember one of the girls whispering, "Pass it down; ask Michaela what did the priest mean by 'original sin'?"

I responded, "It means we're ferociously desirable!" I had no idea what that meant; I was just mimicking my ancestors again.

This is one way of saying I was just passing on our oral tradition. "Ferociously desirable!" Indeed! And my guess is that the ancient Irish women ancestors who were never puritanical, if they could hear Michaela's "ferociously desirable" would smile and say, "Ah yes! You've got that right, Michaela!" *

Wake Time—Storytelling Time

When I was nine years old, I came home from school one day and saw a morose looking gray hearse in front of our house. This was my first encounter with death. My grandfather who lived upstairs had died suddenly. Two days later, they would carry his casket into our house and "Macky" would be waked in our living room. I remember that night of his wake vividly—the smell of the carnations, the flickering red vigil light by Macky's casket, the neighbors coming and going.

My uncle Will Leary had come from Seattle and my uncle Henry Byrne was there too. As a teenager he had run away from an alcoholic father and traveled the world with carnivals. Another relative, Jim Leary, who worked for the railroad, joined the other two uncles in the kitchen. There on the table was a bottle of bourbon and ham sandwiches. When I asked them why they were sitting in the kitchen, they answered they were "waking Macky." And so they sat there all night long, talking and telling stories.

---

* There is no doubt that Michaela's tribal forebears, such as Saint Bridgid and the fifth-century Irish theologian Pelagius, would also have smiled at her answer. His contemporaries, Saints Augustine and Jerome, would not. Augustine dueled with Pelagius about original sin and the theology of grace. Augustine won. "Pelagianism" was condemned.

The misogynist Jerome did not find women desirable at all and excoriated Pelagius for his friendships with "mere women." However, Mary Aileen Schmiel points out that the positive Celtic mindset of Pelagius about the maternal earth, the body and the feminine (if not all of his theology) still endured in early Celtic Christendom. And that story continued to be told and passed on through all the legends about the mighty Saint Brigid.

Uncle Will Leary had traveled the world as an officer in the navy and he had stories to tell of Japan and the Philippines and Uncle Henry Byrne of faraway corners of Mexico.

Between these stories, they told the stories of Macky. "Do you remember when . . ." they would ask each other and then they would remember. They recalled vividly the day that Macky was helping Uncle Will repair a car and how the jack slipped and the car came down on Macky's arm. It had to be amputated and how that changed his life from having an active job on the railroad into having to be a crossing guard at a remote rail crossing called Portal. And they marveled at the good courage Macky showed through the years as he went through the rest of his life with just one arm.

These were marvelous stories that would widen the eyes of any fourth grader. And they were more than that. They were stories of grace at work. While we learned at school the catechism answer to the question "What is grace?" I learned listening at the kitchen table the stories of grace at work in our human stories.

Irish Wakes

In the Celtic tradition, Irish wakes also provided a safety valve. Death was a visitor at the house and was to be acknowledged but not bowed to. Liam Treacy tells the story of the death of a young girl in Dublin in recent times. Her family dug the grave themselves. They carried her casket to the grave on their shoulders. And in a very symbolic way they told the story of her vibrant life by lining the grave with sunflowers. Liam went on to remark: "In the Irish wake and mourning, the soul needs to be accompanied and needs encouragement to move on, and so do the mourners." And so the legendary Irish wakes.

In previous centuries in Ireland the clergy often railed against what they considered to be pagan activities surrounding death and wakes. In days gone by some of their parishioners at wake time might make love in the fields to make sure that death would know that life would triumph after all. Now I know what I could not understand at age nine—that my uncles' storytelling and laughter in the face of death could really be considered not pagan at all, but very Christian. And so storytelling filled with laughter at wake time was also filled with hope.

A Wake Story

There is a story told about an Irish priest arriving for a new assignment. The housekeeper informed him that he would be having a wake that night and a funeral on the morrow.

The deceased's name was Michael and, of course, the new priest knew nothing about him.

So that night, after saying the prayers at the wake, the priest addressed the villagers who had assembled:

"You know, my good people, that I am your new priest and because of that I don't know Michael lyin' here before you. So tomorrow I will be wantin' to say some kind words about Michael at the funeral. I would like your help with this. Think for a moment and then tell me some ways Michael here was a blessing to this community."

This was met with stone silence. So the priest cleared his throat and announced again, "Perhaps you did not understand me. All I want you to tell me is a few ways that Michael was a blessing to you folks who knew him."

Now there was another long silence.

At this point the priest began to get a little angry so he said: "Well, listen now, you are not cooperating with your new priest at all. So I want you to know that I will not be adjourning this wake until you tell me at least one way that Michael was a blessing to this community!"

Now there was an interminable silence, with people coughing, and shifting uneasily in their seats. Finally, a wizened old codger sitting in the back row put up his hand.

"Oh yes, my good man there in the back—tell me one blessing Michael gave to this community."

"Well, . . ." he replied, "his brother was worse!"

In his book *The Catholic Imagination,* Andrew Greeley comments that the Catholic imagination senses grace lurking everywhere and "does not easily give up on the salvation of anyone." Not even on Michael whose only accolade was: "His brother was worse!"

Stories Impact the Imagination

That same year of my grandda's death was my confirmation year. Archbishop James Hugh Ryan, with big bushy eyebrows, was an erudite Irishman who had been chancellor of the Catholic University of America. As a result of a dispute at Catholic University, he left his prestigious post and was named bishop of Omaha in the Midwest. I am still amazed by the fact that his homily at my fourth-grade confirmation is the only homily I ever heard that I can still remember! How could that be? Remembering only one? I think the answer lies in his Irish ability to tell a great story and use a powerful metaphor. He talked about the Mystical Body of Christ. And he used the beautiful metaphor of the vine and the branches. Christ is the vine. We are the branches. Like any good storyteller, he enlivened the image so well that it became imprinted in my memory.

I also remember vividly my grandmother, Maymie McCarthy, painting word pictures for me. She told of standing by the station in Illinois and watching Lincoln's black draped funeral train go by, or of the ride she had as a child when a stage coach took them from Galena, Illinois, out to the frontier and a small town on the riverbank called Omaha. I can still imagine her vivid description of Omaha American Indians peering curiously at her family's arrival and of a friend luckily missing a train whose occupants were later scalped during a foray. She would later write these memories for the local paper at the time of the anniversary of the completion of the transcontinental railroad. But best of all, for me, she stored them in my memory by her storytelling.

The Maternal Line

Interestingly, the written genealogy she left traced not the paternal ancestral line, but rather the maternal ancestral line. "My mother was . . . her mother was . . . etc." There is some hint here of the Irish respect for strong Irish women. Maymie's ancestral line went back through many other Irish names — Byrnes, Coakleys, Greggs, and Hayes — all the way back to seventeenth-century Kanturk in Ireland. In her diary she revealed the names of many gritty and adventurous Irish women. Her recording mentioned five Hayes sisters who all left Ireland in the midst of famine for different ports far away. One of them was Johanna Hayes. Maymie wrote that "she sailed forth for Australia with friends and was never heard from again" — a poignant comment on the Irish diaspora of the nineteenth century. Thomas Kennealy, in his book *The Great Shame and the Triumph of the Irish in the New World*, describes one such journey to Australia as taking a hundred twenty-four days and of coming around the stormy cape and someone being washed overboard. What was Johanna's fate? It is lost in the mists of history and the sadness of the famine.

Seanachies — Irish Storytellers

So these are some of the "seanachies" of my youth, Archbishop Ryan, my uncles, my grandmother, and, most importantly, my own father. Where did their storytelling gifts come from? As I have journeyed back to Ireland and have discovered the seanachies there, I have come to realize that the storytelling gift that was passed down to me from my father came from his father and the rest of my Irish ancestors. For storytelling and good humor are important elements of the Celtic Spirit.

They are priceless secrets, for it is in the telling of our stories that we discover our deepest meaning. This was true for the Jewish people when they gathered for Passover and the youngest child requested: "Tell us the stories of our ancestors and how they escaped from Egypt." Viktor Frankl, a modern Jew who survived the concentration camp, wrote that our deepest human need is our search for meaning. Where else to search for meaning but in our stories?

In the Christian era it was on the road to Emmaus that the disciples traveled and retold the story of the suffering Messiah. It was at a hearthside in an inn over a glass of wine and the breaking of bread that Jesus revealed the deepest meaning of the events that they had witnessed in Jerusalem so few days before.

It is true for the people of Irish descent as well. It was "story" that has sustained our ancestors and illumined their lives during the worst of times and the best of times. We can only know who we really are, where we have come from, and the direction of our destinies by reflecting upon our holy stories. But not just our literal stories. The fables and tales that we imagine also tell us of deeper meanings. The cave of our imagination is a wondrous cavern containing hidden treasures.

Over the centuries, marvelous tales have been handed down from the golden age when Ireland was recognized far and wide as the land of saints and scholars. They have been embellished at the edges just as the scribes embellished the *Book of Kells* with figures and symbols. These stories bear the weight of history but also of magic, imagination, and mystery. For instance, in the telling of the stories of the mighty woman Brigid, she does many imaginative things, such as acting as the nursemaid for Jesus on the flight into Egypt! And in the telling of her stories she takes the place of ancient goddesses who were the stars of previous pre-Christian stories. Listen as a seanachie might embroider a story about the renowned Saint Brigid, the "Mary of the Gael."

Mighty Brigid

Once upon a time, there lived a mighty woman. She walked tall and straight and gave counsel to kings as well as to shepherds with their sheep and milkmaids with their cows. Sometimes she sailed across the fields in her chariot and sometimes she walked with her head bowed in prayer. She possessed a blithe spirit and was attractive in every way. Her fair appearance and prayerful demeanor allured other women toward holiness and the great hero whose cross dwells in the holy circle. And by her word and example she formed them into a Jesus clan.

Not only that, but many men were in awe of her as well. She was worthy to be any king's queen but she was pledged to her hero King.

Then one day, a group of men approached her monastery and asked to speak with her. "Bride of the Gaels, we want to follow you too. Please find room for us in your Jesus clan."

Brigid took this new request to heart, and so at chapter she asked her fellow sisters, "What can we do for the men who seek the peace of prayer in our midst?"

"Nothing!"

"They are too unruly."

"Let them go their own way."

And the prioress had the last word: "Why holy Mother, it's never been done before!"

Such was the response from her sisters.

The next day at midday, Brigid sat by a holy well in meditation. Suddenly, her friends the angels spoke to her: "Brigid, look down into the holy well, for it is in the darkest place that imagination dwells."

So Brigid arose and peered down into the well, but it was black as pitch. She picked up a tiny stone and dropped it down the well. Down, down it fell until a tiny splash echoed back from the depths, but still she could see nothing. Then she picked up another stone and dropped it and at that very moment the noonday sun reached its zenith and a beam shone down into the very depths just as the stone struck the water. And now Brigid could see tiny circle ripples caused by the splash of the stone.

Down in the very depths of imagination, a circle widened for Brigid. Brigid thought about this widening of the circle. "Because it's never been done before," she thought, "does not mean that it can never be done!"

And so it came to be that Saint Brigid came to have a double monastery of both women and men, a monastery with a wider circle. Because of Brigid's great and deep holiness, as deep as the well itself, men and women from all over Eire journeyed to be at her side.

And it is even said by some that one day, in need of a bishop, she so enchanted a bishop with her holiness and learning, that he consecrated her a bishop then and there!

I have heard men say, "That could never be!"

And I have heard women say, "Why not?"

But this I do know: Brigid, Bride of the Gaels, came to be loved and esteemed by all the men and women of Eire. And when pilgrims go today to pray at her holy shrine, a spring flows forth with pristine water. And the pilgrims say their prayers walking round and round in a great circle. And there, in the center of it all, a statue of Brigid carries a shepherd's staff!

The Storytellers' Circles

So seanachies today continue to tell their stories and often embellish them at the edges! Perhaps the oldest of storytelling circles were the primeval hunters returned from the hunt, spinning their tales around the campfire. Storytelling has always been best done around a circle where one story provides the key to another and to another. I remember such a circle when my Fitzgerald uncles would gather. They spun out the tales of their youth so that names and places took life in the fertile imaginations of us children who listened at their knees.

There were colorful names in their stories like Packy McFarland and Wish Larkin, for what are nicknames but the colorful embellishments of storytellers! And they spoke of "the hill" where they were raised, and of their parents, not too long away from ancestors in Ireland, who would roll up the rugs on Saturday evenings and dance the jigs and reels. They spoke of characters of their time, some larger than life. And they were some of the characters themselves—like Uncle Gene who followed the horses and, one time, with his arthritis bothering him greatly, wolfed down a giant pill that a horse trainer friend used to allay the pains of his race horse. Uncle Gene never raced but he did live to tell the story.

We were taken into their stories. They opened up the wider world for us and in doing so they mixed mirth and laughter so that, in the end, we the little ones could peep out at the larger unknown world with anticipation and a sense of wonder and a desire for exploration. From their stories we could dream of adventure and sense that good humor marked their road and could mark ours as well. One story would open up another and often the stories were strung together like rosaries of laughter. If the story line was "food and drink" the stringing together might go this way:

Uncle Clem: "Did you hear about the poor lad who was on his death bed and he could smell the stew cooking on the stove?

"Molly," he said, "can I make one last request of you?"

"What is it, Michael?"

"Could you be after fixin' a bowl of that stew for me?"

"Oh sure, and I couldn't, Michael. Don't ya know it's for your wake!"

Uncle Jim: "Ah, that reminds me of meeting Ryan and asking, 'Did you hear about Cassidy fallin' into the vat at the Guinness factory?'"

"You don't say!" said Ryan. "Did he have a quick death?"

"No, I think he enjoyed the lingerin'. He even went down three times before he yelled for help."

"And that reminds me. . . ."

And so it would go.

In a minor sense, when the uncles told a good story they were seanachies—Irish storytellers. It is interesting that the Irish have a specific word "seanachie" to honor the role of the storyteller. We have no such word in English. We have honored titles such as "computer programmer" and "news commentator," but no special designation for "storyteller." But the Irish do and the storyteller holds a place of honor. Among those honored there is none greater from the past than Peig Sayers and no greater today than Edmund Lenihan.

Peig Sayers

Peig Sayers was a remarkable woman whose life spanned from the nineteenth into the twentieth century. She spent all of her adult life on the Blaskett Islands which lie beyond Dingle off the Kerry coast. One collector of stories gathered three hundred seventy-five tales from her treasure chest of stories. The tradition in Kerry is for the gift of poetry to pass from mother to daughter and the gift of storytelling to pass from the father to the son, but Peig was exceptional in inheriting the seanachie's role from her father.

During the long winters when the Atlantic churned and the north wind rattled the shutters, the islanders without TV, and for a long time even lacking radio, would entertain themselves with storytelling, dance, poetry, and song. And the power of the word was mighty indeed. Peig Sayers could neither read nor write, but true to the ancient Gaelic tradition, she possessed in memory all the words she needed. She knew the stories passed down to her through oral tradition, so highly valued by the Celts. In a lovely book, *Peig Sayers, An Old Woman's Reflections — The Life of a Blaskett Island Storyteller*, some of her stories were transcribed and have finally been saved in print. Not only were her stories interesting in their plots but they were also told with charm and the deft use of symbol and metaphor. In one story she describes the man in the house coming home after having "drunk a drop." His wife, Nora, was waiting for him and Peig remarks that "a woman's tongue is a thing that does not rust!" Only a woman storyteller confidant in her craft could get away with that description.

When one reads the stories of Peig Sayers, the illiterate storyteller, a wonderful grounded spirituality bursts forth in the beauty of the telling and the simple but profound faith that shines through. Peig Sayers is a woman in love with beauty and with God. This is how she describes her growing up:

I was like a little rose in the wilderness I grew up; without for company only those gems that God of Glory created, eternal praise to Him! Every early morning in the summer when the sun would show its face over the top of Eagle Mountain I was often looking at it and at the same time making wonder of the colors in the sky around us. [1]

Peig Sayers' stories were all told in the vernacular Irish. Writing about the Gaelic language, Allistair MacLeod says that some thought that Gaelic speech was the language spoken in the Garden of Eden when God conversed with the angels!

Edmund Lenihan—Storyteller

In our own day, perhaps there is no greater storyteller in Ireland than Edmund Lenihan. Sit by a turf fire at Ennis and let Edmund perform his craft. He stands there, a great bush of dark hair wildly protruding from crown and chin as though it was electrified, shooting out in every direction. And the telling of his stories is just as electric, as if he was plugged into some power source. When he tells the stories of the fairies, you dare not doubt. And when he speaks of Biddy Early, a nineteenth-century healer, she comes alive in the telling. In his book *In Search of Biddy Early*, Edmund testifies that his stories bring to our attention a world not visible to us, but nonetheless very real.

Eddie lives partly in the fairy world and partly in the post-modern age. Only a man of Eddie's gifted tongue could persuade a construction crew to spare a fairy tree that was to be uprooted for "progress." The tree still stands. The road circumvents it.

The Gaelic Way

Patrick Pearse, a progressive educator at his Saint Enda's School in Dublin, before leading the 1916 Easter rising, recognized the importance of storytelling in his own life:

It is a long time since I was first attracted by the Gaelic way of educating children. One of my oldest recollections is of a kindly gray-haired seanachie, a woman of my mother's people, telling tales by the kitchen fireplace.

Today, the storyteller's circle has been replaced with virtual reality games and the constant cascade of images from TV where everything has to be visible. No longer is the circle of storytelling elders passing on a heritage from generation to generation and that is a loss. However, the stories to be found in literature still remain as popular as ever and there the presence of the Irish storytellers endures. The three top novels of the twentieth century selected by the Modern Library are by Irish authors: *Ulysses* by James Joyce, *The Great Gatsby* by F. Scott Fitzgerald, and *A Portrait of an Artist as a Young Man* by Joyce. And, in the genre of the written short story, the Irish presence excels.

The Word Made Flesh

"In the beginning was the Word . . ." Thus begins the prologue of John's gospel. And the "Word was made flesh." In some real analogical sense, the word of faith sometimes is made flesh and comes alive through storytelling! We have no better witness to this than Jesus himself. Were he walking the earth today how would he communicate? Would he have a weekly TV show in which he would ask million-dollar catechism questions—the prize being salvation? Would he read encyclical letters? No. He would tell stories. Ask any preacher when the assembly perks up, pays most attention, strains to listen. This happens only when a good story is told. Jesus was a superb storyteller. He harvested his stories from everyday life—the sower in the field, the woman searching for a coin, the lost sheep.

We need to let Jesus be our seanachie! We need to enter into his stories and place ourselves within them in our own imagination. Be the woman at the well. Be the thief on the cross. Be the man born blind. When we meditate and place ourselves into the stories they have the power to touch us at a very deep level. And they are always good news for our souls.

Thomas Merton in his seminal book, *The Seven Storey Mountain*, wrote that the only way to live is to live in a world that is charged with the presence and reality of God. And this is what stories of grace call us to—God's gracious presence at work in our everyday world.

John Shea, a consummate Irish American storyteller, puts it another way. He writes that stories of the human spirit help us to see from the viewpoint of the soul.

Stories of the Human Spirit Can Illumine Faith

In recent years, there are three groups that I am familiar with who provide shelter where space can be carved out for the telling of our stories—RENEW groups, the Rite of Christian Initiation of Adults, and the Recovery groups. Over the years, I have participated in a number of RENEW groups in several parishes. In the RENEW process, a safe space is provided where people are allowed to share some of their personal faith stories with others listening intently without interruption or even comment. Like rain upon fertile ground, the stories are allowed to sink in.

The RENEW groups are usually limited to eight persons. What the participants experience is a storytellers' circle, which is not really available anywhere else in our hyphenated world. People rush about sharing millions of cryptic messages but too seldom take the time to share their stories.

I shall never forget Peter, an eighty-year-old man who facilitated a RENEW group made up mostly of elderly persons. With failing eyesight, Peter would have to get up from the group, go out to the kitchen, and hold his guide book up to the window in order to read the instructions for the group.

Within the group, however, Peter needed no such light to share his own experiences from his faith journey. These stories enlightened his soul and shone out in his telling. Peter was an immigrant and I shall always remember him describing the *Angelus* being rung in his native village as the farmers in the fields would hear the chiming echoing back from the hills. Upon hearing it they would drop to their knees and say their prayers. A faith story, a beautiful image, told with simplicity.

Such stories are not just stored in the file cabinet of the brain but rather occupy a hallowed place in the human heart. Unfortunately, there are stories of lived faith like Peter's all around us. For the most part, they remain books unopened. Too often, we walk through life keeping our deepest and most meaningful stories to ourselves.

RCIA

In the Rite of Christian Initiation of Adults, the scripture stories interweave with the journey stories of the participants with all trails coming together in Christ. The journey of the participants resembles in many ways the journey of the two disciples on the road to Emmaus.

What I have observed in both of these groups is that the participants become refreshed and their hopes rekindled when they listen to how God's amazing grace has entered into one another's stories. And these stories perhaps never would be told were it not for RENEW and RCIA providing a safe place for personal storytelling.

"Good morning. My name is John and I am an alcoholic."

Another successful storytellers' circle is that of the recovery groups. Here, truth is faced head on. Here, the stories are tales of the heroine's and hero's quests in a very real life because they all tell of journeys, of facing the dragon or hitting rock bottom, only to be turned around aided by a higher power.

The Power of Storytelling

When we explore the power of storytelling we discover immense benefits. Sometimes our stories provide mirth and laughter in the midst of a tearful world. Sometimes they help us discover the deeper meanings in our lives. When told to children, stories light up their imaginations and pass on a heritage from their ancestors. Imaginative stories have the power to help us explore the depth, the nuance, and the ambiguities of life. Fundamentalists who look at life in terms of black and white are not the best tellers of stories.

Messy people familiar with the gray areas are. For they know that our stories weave through gray areas and take paradoxical twists and turns. They know that God sometimes writes straight with crooked lines. Storytelling that plumbs the human spirit can also illumine and encourage our faith life. These are all very good reasons why we can profit from a rediscovery of the Celtic gift and secret of the story.

Prayer

O God, help me to know
that I am a part of the great story of evolution.
My origins are one with the sun and the stars.
My body is made of stardust.
Through this great story
and the unfolding story of my own life,
make me aware that there is more to life
than meets the eye.
And when I hear the gospel story
may I be there through holy imagination
to sit like Mary at the foot of the Lord,
knowing no better story than his.

Journal Option:
If I were to write my story, what chapter am I in?
Does it have enough laughter?
Too much sorrow or tragedy?
What can I do to make it a happier and more fulfilling story?

Notes: [1] Peig Sayers, *An Old Women's Reflections, The Life of a Blasket Island Storyteller,* translated from the Irish by Seamus Ennis and introduced by W. R. Rogers, Oxford University Press, Oxford, 1962, p. 81.

CHAPTER SIX

The Beauty of the Poetic Word and Creative Imagination

The Sixth Secret of the Celtic Spirit

The Poetic Word

Inaugural podium glaring white,
their breaths—white crystals.
Sun slanted in January sky.
The old warrior girded in black.
White, silk scarf ruffled.
"Hail to the chief! Farewell!"
Words echo back, echo back.

He reined impetuous Patton.
Cajoled the haughty Monty
and risked all to win
on bloody Norman shores.
Now he desists, pulls back,
lets go the oval grandeur.
Words echo back, echo back.

The brash young Gael
head hatless, hair disheveled.
Once a yachtsman, then a sailor,
from so very small a ship
sunk in vast and perilous seas.
He now boards the ship of state.
Words echo back, echo back.

This young usurper Celt
first of his kind to best the Wasps
from both sides of Boston tracks.
Sweet speech from Honey Fitz,
measured cadence from Harvard Yard,

does so solemnly swear.
Words echo back, echo back.

The old poet laureate
white maned before the flag.
Who else but a Gael
would place an ancient bard
between the old warrior
and his New Frontier?
Words echo back, echo back.

"Ask not what your country can do
but what you can do"—an echo.
Now borne away in motorcade.
But all too soon, clip clop, clip clop,
of Black Jack—now riderless—
and the caisson's mournful creak.
Words echo back, echo back.

When his ancestral peoples
sailed from out of Wexford
famine ravished and ill shod
they brought no baggage
little else but dreams,
and the power of their words.
Words echo back, echo back.

Before that, for eight hundred years
rebellions quashed so many times.
All that was left, the power of words,
dying heroes' last words,
whispered behind hedgerows,

furtive speech in pub and glen.
Words echo back, echo back.

In houses of memory
poets as if slain warriors
lay in the pregnant, holy dark
musing, dreaming, birthing,
drawing forth primeval images
linking verse to verse.
Words echo back, echo back.

From the bright inaugural stand
back through all the misty ages
from the Druids' sacred groves
and the monks' corbelled huts
the poetic words endure.
Cached away—heart treasures.
Words echo back, echo back.

The sixth secret of the poetic word is closely related to the fifth secret of storytelling. Not only have the Irish been great storytellers, their speech also sparkles with the poetic word. The Irish Celts have always delighted in the beauty and power of the poetic words that spring forth from fertile Gaelic imaginations. The gift for metaphor and for colorful speech is an attribute of the Irish that stretches back through history to the days when the ancient Celts possessed a great oral culture and the bards made speech always colorful and often entertaining.

The beauty of the poetic word and creative imagination is the sixth secret of the Celtic Spirit. It has leaped across the centuries and was brought to the New World by the Irish immigrants, poor in worldly goods, but rich in the gift of gab—in the colloquial some called it "Blarney." But it was more than that. It was also the gift of making speech vivid and often poetic.

The Poetic Irish American Moment

I watched the presidential inauguration of 1960 on black and white TV. For myself and other Irish Americans, John F. Kennedy marked a poetic moment that signaled that the Irish immigrants had finally arrived as Americans. I also watched his funeral a few short years later. About his tragic death, perhaps no one summed up the feelings of Irish Americans better than Daniel Patrick Moynihan in an interview on WTOP radio, November 23, 1962: "I guess there is no point in being Irish if you don't know that the world will break your heart some day."

At JFK's swearing in, things were done as ancient Irish chieftains would have done. The new leader had a poet laureate at his side. So too at his death his brother turned to the poetic word to mourn his passing. At such moments of national crisis, or indeed at moments of personal mourning, the soul turns to poetry. It is precisely symbol, metaphor, poetry, that stretches to bridge the gap between mortality and immortality, between hope and despair.

The Poetic Word and Politics

JFK knew the power of both the poetic and the political word. Perhaps he knew it by osmosis, for it is the Celtic gift, the Celtic heritage, perhaps even, in the language of Jung, "an archetype" in the collective Irish imagination. When his ancestors were denied any power of ascendancy, they held to themselves the power of words. Not only did they possess the poetic word, they also excelled at the political word.

George Reedy, Lyndon Johnson's former press secretary, wrote in his book *From The Ward To The White House: The Irish In*

American Politics, that in the old country the Irish became supremely skilled at conducting their own affairs while seeming to leave full authority to a hostile power. This ability to speak their own words in small gatherings in their pubs, right under the noses of their English occupiers, allowed them to control their local affairs despite being occupied. Reedy sees this facility as the most useful skill the Irish immigrants brought to America. Tip O'Neill once said, "All politics is local." The Irish knew that all along.

Even when their native Gaelic language was taken away from them, a fate few other peoples have known, the gift for images, metaphor, and poetic word was translated into their expressions in English. Paradoxically, when they arrived in the New World, they were one step ahead of other arrivals with their knowledge of English. And they still possessed in their collective unconscious the echoes of their ancestors.

So no matter where the nineteenth-century immigrants landed, they brought with them poetic spirits that echoed all the way back to the Druids. As Morgan Llywelyn tells us in her book *Druids,* the principal obligation of the Druids was to keep mankind, earth, and the otherworld in harmony. Where there is harmony, there is poetry, for the poet takes the jumbled words, the chattered words, the fractured words and mends them into harmony.

The Flow of Words

It is one of the marvels of history that Druidry gave way almost graciously to Christianity. And might some of it be explained by the Druids' love for the poetic word? Like a river receiving a tributary, the words of the old pagan Celts flowed and merged into the stream of the psalms and gospels. From his Druid ancestors, Saint Colmcille inherited a reverence for the poetic word. When the status of poets in Ireland was threatened he successfully pleaded their cause and defended their rights. And no doubt when Colmcille prayed the psalms or read Isaiah, these ancient poetic words were balm for his soul. Surely the monastic sons of Colmcille would have carried on his reverence for the cadence and flow of words.

Imagine Colmcille going forth from his beloved cell in the woods of Derry to found a monastery in the rugged and beautiful glens of Donegal. Imagine years later his monks assembling there for prayer:

> The year is A.D. 600. It is Advent, and the monks, as did their Druid ancestors, are waiting for the return of the sun after the longest night of the year. But they wait for more— for the coming of the Son, the second person of the sacred three who for them is the light of the world. Some of the monks themselves are probably converts from Druidry.
>
> Before the dawn, in the cold, damp month of December, the monks rise from their beds of straw placed in their small individual huts. They robe themselves in coarse wool robes. They move in silence toward their chapel, perhaps a corbelled stone beehive structure with a capacity of no more than ten or twelve. (There are no cathedrals in Ireland in the year 600.)
>
> They enter into the small chapel hooded. There is a lectern in the center flanked by two candles. Upon it rests a Psalter, large calfskin pages containing mostly psalms with some readings from the other scriptures. It is highly prized and is placed in a position of honor. Its Latin text is precious and copied by hand. Bear in mind that it has only been about two hundred years since Saint Jerome translated the scriptures into Latin and hand-copied texts are still rare. The candlelight casts a soft glow upon the parchment. And the monks' shadows weave along the rough rock walls—stone upon stone without mortar.
>
> The monks gather in a semicircle, for the Celts loved to pray in a circle. They pull back their hoods revealing their tonsured heads trimmed in the Druid fashion, shaved in front, long hair in back. In rhythmic chant their leader sings out, *Deus in adjutorium meum intende* ("O God, come to our assistance!"). And then, as the monks make a profound

bow, *Gloria Patri et Filio et Spiritui Sancto!* ("Glory to the Father and to the Son and to the Holy Spirit!"). A synonym for glory is beauty. So "Beauty to the Holy Three!" Glory as beauty comes easily to the chanters, for they are in love with the beauty of the land around them.

And worship of a holy three comes easy for the chanters, for is not the number three the sacred Druid number? And then the psalms of David, the poet-warrior, echo back and forth from one semicircle to the other. They need no book in hand, for all the psalms are memorized just as their pagan ancestors memorized all they needed to know.

How David's words are in tune with their own Druid past, which reverenced the sacred source in nature and believed that Lugh, the God of the Sun, reached down his hands into human affairs! And so they chant:

> The heavens are telling the glory of God;
> and the firmament proclaims his handiwork.
> Day by day pours forth speech,
> and night to night declares knowledge.
> There is no speech, nor are there words;
> their voice is not heard;
> yet their voice goes out through all the earth,
> and their words to the end of the world.
> In the heavens he has set a tent for the sun,
> which comes out like a bridegroom from his
> wedding canopy,
> and like a strong man runs its course with joy.
> Its rising is from the end of the heavens,
> and its circuit to the end of them;
> and nothing is hid from its heat. (Psalm 19:1–6)

And when they finish chanting the psalms, they sit down to listen to the Advent reading from the poetic, Advent prophet Isaiah. And when they hear it, they even imagine that Isaiah was a Celt too. How these words are dear to their old Druid hearts and their new Christian spirit!

So one monk, chosen as lector, goes to the lectern and proclaims:

A reading from the prophet Isaiah:

The wolf shall live with the lamb, the leopard shall lie down with the kid; the calf and the lion and the fatling together, and a little child shall lead them. The cow and the bear shall graze, their young shall lie down together; and the lion shall eat straw like the ox. The nursing child shall play over the hole of the asp, and the weaned child shall put its hand on the adder's den. They will not hurt or destroy on all my holy mountain; for the earth will be full of the knowledge of the LORD as the waters cover the sea. (Isaiah 11:6–8)

When the lector put down the calfskin Psalter, he must have been touched in many ways. Isaiah wrote with the heart of a poet and the poet was of equal honor to the warrior in many of their clans. Also, Isaiah's reconciling of opposites would not have been difficult for them, for they were not dualistic in their heritage — dividing things up as the Romans would. Not only that, did not their own founder Colmcille insist that any wounded animal or bird was to be treated as kin and given food and shelter at the monastery? So these powerful images of Isaiah would find a warm welcome in their fertile imaginations. They would be consoling images.

But these newly minted monks would also be challenged by the ending of Isaiah's passage proclaiming no ruin on the holy mountain, for they were the sons of warriors, or perhaps even former warriors themselves and they had seen ruins on their mountains from various clan clashes and cattle raids. And this is where their challenge of conversion lay—to turn the energy of conflict into zeal for the Lord.

Finally, the words of Isaiah proclaiming that the earth would be filled with the knowledge of the Lord, and Isaiah's words that "blessed on the mountains are the footsteps of those who bring good news," would send them forth eager to do their daily work of preserving the sacred words of scripture in their scriptorium, but also of putting on to parchment the ancient poetry of their ancestors.

These ancient monks built no great edifices nor beautiful cathedrals. Indeed, even today as pilgrims visit the great European cathedrals at York, Notre Dame, Chartres, or Cologne, no one travels to Ireland to enter beautiful churches. The beauty of the Irish-Celtic Spirit rests in words, not brick and mortar. The most revered ancient Christian treasure in Ireland is a beautiful book of words—the *Book of Kells*—on view in Trinity College Library. On its pages the ancient monks played with words, embellishing the letters with curls and swirls and spirals. The medium became a part of the message. From the Celtic imagination words were to flash forth in an illumined and beautiful fashion.

An ancient Irish scribe would write of his own efforts: "A stream of the wisdom of Blessed God springs forth from my brown shapely hands . . . in the page it squirts its draught."

The Beauty of Penmanship

The beauty that can spring from the handwritten texts is perhaps one of the casualties of our cyber world. E-mail has replaced a great deal of letter writing. In the last century, penmanship was an important skill in order to communicate legibly. And in many ways the penmanship revealed the personality of the person writing. For all of the blessings of increased communication that e-mail brings, it lacks the beauty of the handwritten word. In the nineteenth century, a handwritten letter, sealed with a wax seal, was a work of art. No e-mail could ever come close to a handwritten love letter.

Ronald Reagan, like Kennedy, another descendant of the ancient Irish, over a long lifetime wrote hundreds of lyric love letters to his wife Nancy. They are now preserved in the Reagan Presidential Library. On presenting them to the library, Nancy Reagan remarked that nothing gives the "flavor of a person" like a handwritten message.

E-mail because of its speedy transmission can also result in a lot of sloppy punctuation. In our modern cyber world whatever is functional and fast will usually win out over that which takes more time to be beautiful. Rollo May, in his book *My Quest for Beauty*, writes that we are enslaved to a money-minded culture and as a result suppress our hunger for beauty. Brevity supplants beauty. Notice in our rush to send the message, few e-mails begin with the formal "Dear . . ." Such a word as "Dear" sends a powerful personal message. It is a blessing, an affirmation, and a warm greeting. When we lose such endearing touches we remove any depth and replace it with shallowness. Every word counts. Subtraction of words may be more efficient but it is seldom more endearing. The *Carmina Gadelica,* a treasure house of ancient blessings translated from the Gaelic, offers a beautiful blessing for words:

> Sweetness be in my mouth,
> Wisdom be in my speech.

For the Celts, words are like sparks in the dark—darting hither, thither, and yon—capable of sparking a blaze of love, the surprise of wonder, or the mirth of laughter. Pete Hamill writes that the use of language is a "form of magic."

Words are a benefice, a rich heritage of a long oral culture. And the poorest of the poor can be rich in words. Ireland never produced a Shakespeare but it is worth noting that in the years when Shakespeare lifted his quill and touched it to immortality, Oliver Cromwell lifted his sword and torch in Ireland, scorching the earth, slashing and burning the native Gaelic culture and ancient Celtic Christian heritage. In his aftermath, all that was left to the Irish were whispered words. About the only written treasure Cromwell spared was the *Book of Kells*. It was too beautiful for even the iconoclast Cromwell to destroy.

This is why the Celtic secret of the beauty of the poetic word and elegance of beautifully inscribed words such as are found in the *Book of Kells* is a secret worth rediscovering in our time. And this may be happening. Donald Jackson, calligrapher and longtime scribe to Queen Elizabeth's Crown office, has fulfilled a dream by hand copying and illuminating a two-foot-tall and three-foot-wide vellum Old and New Testament Bible for the monks of Saint John's Abbey at Collegeville, Minnesota. It comprises seven volumes and contains a hundred and sixty illuminations.

When asked about the payoff from such a long and intensive labor, Jackson replied: "I want people to say 'Ah' when they look at the *Saint John's Bible,* not only because they are dazzled by the gold and vermilion, or awed by the calligraphy, but because they discover something inside themselves, something they may not have known was there."

No doubt the ancient Irish scribes who labored over vellum with the same inks and pens that Jackson is using would say "Ah!" as well. And they might add that the something to be discovered from a book of beauty is faith itself.

If Europe's cathedrals sprang up from the roots of peasants' faith, the beautiful words of the Irish flowered forth from the precious old sod. David Abram, in his insightful book *The Spell of the Sensuous — Perception and Language in a More-Than-Human World,* writes that language is rooted in earth. He says that the locale, the place itself, speaks through the poets' or writers' words. There is even an Old Irish saying: "The land sings its own song."

In Ireland the earth speaks and sings!
My flesh comes from this land,
just as sure as the daisies,
as sure as the grass,
from the reek's high brow,
to the fertile valleys.
My blood from holy wells,
my spirit from soaring birds.
And my beautiful words
from the orchids springing up
'tween cracks of Burren rock!

As one travels throughout Ireland, the tone and lilt and inflections vary from city to countryside, from oceanside to farmstead, reflecting in some way the flavor of the land. What is common to all of these brogues is colorful, earthy language that carries with it the lilt of music and the rhythm of poetry. When I listened to Jimmy Carr, a farmer and local historian in Donegal as he lovingly described the blessed turf where Colmcille walked, there was an almost musical delight in the lilt of his words. In his speech, there flowed an undertone of laughter, which tossed up the words like froth from the sea.

The Musical Delight of Words

In James Stephens' *Irish Fairy Stories,* a debate occurs about what is the finest music in the world. Fionn the chief settles the argument: "The music of what happens, that is the finest music in the world."

The musical delight of words and rhythm is learned early on in Erin. Michael Gibbons tells the story of himself and his six-year-old daughter. He was giving a lecture on archeology. She is present and gets bored after two minutes. So she tromps up from the audience and sits down right before him on the stage. She looks up at him and then she starts to sing. He whispers to her: "You're making noise." She looks up at him and responds: "No I am not. I'm singing to you! They won't mind!"

Even the Profane Is Softer!

Listen to conversations in pubs and the expressions are colorful and mixed with metaphor. Even in their profanity, the words take on an air of mischief and seem less dire and threatening than curses heard elsewhere. Listen long enough and you will hear lots of the "F" word, but even here, the Irish seem to soften it by changing the Anglo Saxon ending "uck," which is not pleasant to the ear to "oookin', " which seems more naughty than nasty.

Peig Sayers, the Blaskett Island storyteller, recounts a conversation when a visitor remarked that the people of her island have a fine gift of cursing. She replied: "I make little of them, for if the blessings come from the heart, I don't care where the curses come from."

Among the Irish, conversation is an art form that weaves poetry and metaphor through its fabric. And the Irish even have a word, "craic," for those times when good conversation fills the air. Here are segments of one evening dinner party conversation at the home of Colm and Veronica MacGuire where *craic* was in abundance:

"Veronica, has the flu come to your house yet?"

"Sure, not at all, not at all. And even if the Federal Express man brought it, we just wouldn't accept it. We'd just refuse it at the door and send it back!"

"Speakin' of comin' to the door, did I tell you that when an Irish nun, no relative of ours, visited my sister in Glasgow, my brother-in-law looked at her and exclaimed, 'Sure and you're the spittin' image of Veronica's sister back home!' And then my sister says, 'Sure'n, our father must have had a bicycle!'"

"And the nun was not likin' that response at all. Sure she had an expression on her face like she had been hit by a dead cat!"

"Ah, do your hear that music in the background playin'? It's the Irish tenors. Sure when I hear that I get glory bumps on my arms!"

And later, over wine: "Ya know, at Cana, the simple water heard the Master's voice and blushed a bright red hue—becomin' the very best of wines!"

Here are other random poetic words and expressions I gleaned from conversations and print as I journeyed through Ireland:

Pub Talk:
They were so poor they could not afford a second name for
    their son.
The moon is the lamp of the poor.

Long roads and stony ditches and here's to nice girls and
to hell with riches!

Better a smaller portion with a blessing than too large a
portion with a curse.

You have to say nice things about the dead. They can't
speak for themselves.

Ah, the gulf stream like a lover kisses the Irish shore and
warms it.

The only good thing in Limerick are the roads that take
you to Tipperary.

You can tell a man by the way he wears his hat.

Ah, there will be skin and hair flyin' today at the hurling
match!

Hurling! The clash of the ash!

People of the mountains dance up and down.

People of the valleys dance all around.

There's many a good tune played on an old fiddle.

On a graveyard stone:
Asleep in Jesus . . . blessed sleep!
From which none ever awakes to weep!

It's very difficult to get out of this world alive.

What's meant for me will not pass me by.

I knew him when he didn't have an arse to fill his pants.

I never went to school myself but I often met with scholars
on the road.

Nicknames for Statues in Dublin:
Goddess of the River Liffey: "The Floozie in the Jacuzzi."
Molly Molone: "The Tart with the Cart."
William Butler Yeats: "The Lank by the Bank."
You know a cell phone can turn into a jail cell.
To balance a long stick, you must go to the middle.
A good story takes three weeks to tell.
Waves will rise in silent water.

There is no guile in the young,
. . . and in that, they come close to the sun.

In conversation the adjectives of the speakers
often express their Irish poetic spirits.
They are more often than not vivid and passionate:
A mighty woman!
A savage storm!
A fierce performance!
A brilliant conversation!

And when asked about the power of religion:
Religion is for those afraid of hell.
Spirituality is for those of us who have been there.
You must be willing to go down into dark places.
Religion names God in people's lives.
Pain is the touchstone of spiritual growth.

And when I searched for the "Celtic Spirit"
and what it was like to be Irish,
these were some of the beautiful answers I found:
Kerry: "It's a feeling of being at home with everything."
Sheila Tiernan: "It's to be blest even in the midst of
    sorrow."
Terrence Sheehy: "To know the language of all living things."
Traditional: "Strength in the arm. Truth on the lips.
    Courage in the heart."
The Claddagh Ring: The hand—Friendship, the Crown—
    Loyalty, the Heart—Love.
Caitlin Matthews in *The Encyclopedia of Irish Wisdom:*
    "Central to Irish belief—honor for distant ancestors, a
    sense of family, and an abiding connection to the land."

The Earth Speaks

Just as the Eiffel Tower sprang up from the industrial age of the
old world and skyscrapers sprang up from the capitalism of the

new world, so too the power and beauty of the poetic word sprang up in Ireland from the people's rootedness in the old sod itself. For in Ireland, the land speaks to the poetic heart. It evokes poetry. It has been so since the epic myths of the pre-Christian Cuchulainn, down through Colmcille, the poetic bards, to the more recent times of Yeats, Lady Gregory, and to the new century through such writers as Seamus Heaney, Thomas Nolan, and Nuala ni Dhomhnaill.

Postmodern Connectors to the Poetic Word

Besides Seamus Heaney, winner of the Nobel Poetry prize in 1995, there are other younger writers at the turn of this new century, such as Nuala and Thomas Nolan who connect so very well to the ancient Irish tradition of the poetic word. Nuala writes in the ancient Gaelic, the Irish language that is experiencing a revival of sorts in the twenty-first century. Her writing is earthy and methaphorical. Writing in an article titled "The Lingual Ideal in the Poetry of Nuala ni Dhomhnaill" in the journal *Eire-Ireland*, Deborah McWilliams comments that Nuala's reference to ancient female fertility goddesses captures the impulses of a maternal earthly realm. Deborah also credits Nuala with reviving the premodern Irish belief in the existence of two realms of being—the worldly or natural and the preternatural which the ancient Irish believed flowed together.

"She"—The Old Sod

Nuala's poetry is vividly erotic and springs forth from the fertile earth—the old sod. And the "old sod" is personified as feminine. Nuala's erotic imagery "mimics the ancestors." Thomas Cahill, in *How the Irish Saved Civilization*, points out that going all the way back to the Irish prose epic, *The Cattle Raid of Cooley*, the sexual frankness in the speech of the Irish characters is more direct than anything to be found in classical literature.

So Nuala honors the female body as a personification of the Irish curved hillsides and fertile fields. She has not invented this.

Ask a farmer in Kerry what are the names of the two mountains side by side and he will answer as his ancient ancestors did, "Why sure, they are the paps of Enu!" (The breasts of the goddess Enu.) In giving a critique of Nuala's work, McWilliams credits Nuala with providing insight into the importance of women in early Ireland.

Thomas Nolan

Thomas Nolan expresses in a high degree the Irish gift of poetic expression and he writes prose that is creatively imaginative and metaphorical. More than that, he possesses the indomitable Celtic spirit that will not be ground away by the most difficult of hardships. As Sheila Tiernan in Ennis remarked to me when I asked her about the Celtic spirit: "The Irish spirit means to be blest in the midst of sorrow."

At his birth Thomas Nolan was deprived of oxygen for two hours. As a result, he was paralyzed. He has had to write by having another person hold his head while he taps the typewriter with a stick attached to his forehead. He calls it his "unicorn stick." It took him twelve years and a half-million strokes to write his first novel, *The Banyon Tree*. In this remarkable story, the first chapter tells the tale of a woman churning butter. That is it. However the telling is so rich and vivid that it rivets the reader's attention. Out of the dark cave of his imagination he has mined gold.

The Cave of Darkness

In the days of the pre-Christian mythic gods and goddesses, and even far into the Christian era, Irish poets carried in their memories the poetic words and mythic tales. They honored the holy darkness by going into the dark of houses of memories. There in the holy, pregnant dark their imaginations were unfettered. A master poet was expected to enter into a trance for nine whole days and nights! Imagination flourished in the dark. In our modern cyber world, few of us are ever in the dark and not much is left to our imagination if our waking hours are taken up with television. There is a secret to be learned in our time from darkness and from silence. Out of the silence of the meditating Celtic bards came a folklore which William Butler Yeats described as contributing to the quick intelligence and abundant imaginations of the Irish country people.

My own first personal experience of images and even poetry emerging from the "holy dark" occurred when I was three years old! There were no other children my age. I played alone until one day two playmates came to join me. They came walking out of my imagination. Their names were Kido and Kay Cook—lovely poetic names for lively playmates. I entered easily into their world. My parents were kind to Kay Cook and Kido and would ask me to tell them about my two friends. That went on for a while but eventually I got so much into their world that my parents may have worried about me going off of the deep end, and so they made an effort to demythologize Kido and Kay Cook.

One evening they asked if I could take them to see Kido and Kay Cook.

I said, "I guess so but we'll have to go in the car because they don't live near here."

"OK," they said and so we got all dressed up and got into the car.

After we drove around for a while, I said: "They live in that house over there."

So, my father pulled up the car in front and suggested we go into the house to meet them.

"OK."

So up we went on the porch and my father rang the bell.

No answer.

Much to my satisfaction, I announced: "They must not be home."

And I no doubt breathed a sigh of relief. My imaginary world was undisturbed.

The ancient Irish would have certainly understood the presence of Kay Cook and Kido because for them imagination was a real world, a land to explore, a source of energy. There were other experiences of early childhood that entered like seeds into my own imagination. One would be my parents taking me to see the Christmas crib. Andrew Greeley—the brilliant priest, sociologist, novelist, theologian, and Irish American—has written that faith itself is not just nourished in the intellect but also grows in the dark cave of the imagination. That is the land where images come alive.

Poetry and Our Spiritual Lives

Our inner spirit hungers for the poetic word. Reading through the offerings by Retreats International, they list "Reading Poetry for Spiritual Growth" and they describe the nourishing aspects of poetry this way:

> . . . as a gift of the Spirit that enriches our quest for fuller life in God. The course offers a unique approach to reading poetry as a *lectio divina,* and a chance to share the fruits of individual meditation on selected poems. Whether poetry is a new acquaintance or a longtime friend, it will be offered as a fresh resource for spiritual discernment and growth.

Poetry is a gift of the spirit. It is worth noting that the longest uninterrupted prayer of Western civilization is the poetry of the psalms. Some of the poetic psalms were composed and sung by King David. For millennia before Christ they were chanted in the synagogues. They were the poetry that Jesus knew and prayed. And in Western monasticism, day by day down through the centuries of the last two millennia, they have been sung in choir at various hours of each day by monks around the world. In the golden age of Ireland the psalms mixed and mingled with the sights and sounds of nature. Their chanting sewed together work, play, and rest into one great tapestry of prayer. Thus, Colmcille prayed:

That I might bless the Lord
Who conserves all —
Heaven with its countless bright orders,
Land, strand and flood,
That I might search the books all
That would be good for any soul;
At times kneeling to beloved Heaven
At times psalm singing;
At times contemplating the King of Heaven,
Holy the Chief;
At times at work without compulsion,
This would be delightful;
At times picking kelp from the rocks
At times fishing
At times giving food to the poor
At times in my monastery cell.

Saint Colmcille

And today the twenty-first-century revival of interest in chant reveals a hunger for prayerful poetry and a hunger for contemplative beauty. But not all prayer involves words. Contemplative prayer honors silence. But when words are used it would seem that prayer demands beautiful words. For to adore the creator is to pay homage to the beauty of God. Is it not also true that the poetic words of Sacred Scripture make the deepest impression on our souls and on our memories? Such beautiful words of Jesus about the lilies of the fields, a fountain springing up to eternal life, or the blessings of the Beatitudes energize our spiritual lives.

Today, in our Western world we need to rediscover the beauty of the poetic word. If we do, perhaps speed for efficiency might be balanced with taking time for beauty. Colorful and imaginative conversation might replace passive viewing. Course speech and dumbed-down discourse might be replaced by poetic words. And our prayer lives, which can become dry and routine, might be nourished by poetry and by images. The medium enhances the message.

Andrew Greeley, writing about the Irish imagination in his book *The Catholic Imagination,* stresses its roots in the earth and says that the Irish imaginative spirit that comes forth in words will always be "convoluted, intricate and above all exuberantly playful." The earth speaks through us. The words we say are us. The images we entertain are us. The Spirit dwells deep in our imaginative dark. A person of wit speaks in a playful way which is joyful. A person of peace speaks in a peaceful way which is calming. A person of hate speaks in a hateful way which is ugly.

The Most Beautiful Words

John was our chief usher. He always wore a smile and his spirit was unflagging but his heart was not. It was dying a little every day. And so, as he was waiting his turn for a heart transplant, one day he gave me the following little quote which had moved him to be even more affirming with words to others than he usually was:

> Suppose one morning you never wake up, do all your friends know that you love them? I was thinking I could die today, tomorrow, or next week and I wondered: "Do I have any wounds needing to be healed or friendships that need rekindling?" There are three words needing to be said. Sometimes the words "I love you!" can heal and bless. Let every one of your friends know you love them. You would be amazed at what those three little words and a smile can do. Just in case I die tomorrow, I LOVE YOU.

These three words really are the most beautiful words in the world. The theology of the Evangelist John assures us that "in the beginning was the Word!" And John, as well as our own imaginations and poetic sense, assures us that the "Word" was beautiful! So shall we be if our words are beautiful—our images sublime! We would be wise if we did not keep them damned up waiting for other days to speak them.

Words Like Water

Our words are like water
cascading down,
splashing upon rocks,
leaving no imprint,
quickly flowing away.

Sometimes like gentle dew
alighting with tender touch.
Subtle, whispering, soothing,
so lightly borne.
Never bending fragile leaves.

Sometimes a torrent
sweeping away silence.
Rushing, rushing
too much, too many, too fast.
Filling days with cell phone chatter.

Sometimes a dancing stream
rippling with mirth —
good "craic," frowns to smiles
tossing up the froth of laughter
washing away fatigue.

Too often a reservoir of words
filled with great potential
but damned in, saved.
Never loosed, never spoken.
Leaving thirsty hearts empty.

But the best of words
echo on forever.
Melting icy glaciers,
singing down the mountains,
making fertile every promise.

Prayer

O God, just as water was turned to wine at Cana,
turn my tepid words into wine of lasting vintage.
Empower me to speak words of beauty —
bringing peace, affirmation, and joy.
Let them echo through the lives of all whom I love.

Journal Option:
I need to speak . . .

Notes: Scripture quotes from New Revised Standard Version, Division of Christian Education of the National Council of Churches of Christ in the United States of America, Collins, 1989.

CHAPTER SEVEN

The Holy Circle — The Dance Around the Celtic Cross

The Seventh Secret of the Celtic Spirit

Tory

Last look back at Erin
at the edge of yesterday
and all tomorrows.
Winds lift shadow quilts
off the sleepy mountains.
Buoys blink—all's well.
Small waves teeter totter,
up, down, cavorting with the shore.
May's breezes flirt and dance,
winter's gray cloak cast away.
White birds flutter.
Erigal mighty mountain!
Music echoes back from Tory
across the golden strand.
Last king in Erin,
three gold rings accoutered,
"Up!"—Join the dance!

A seventh secret of the Celtic Spirit is the image that appears on hillsides, in old church yards, and in ancient burial grounds all around Ireland. It is the image of a spirited circle—seemingly dancing around a holy cross. Only in Celtic lands do we find the cross encircled. Why? How did this come to be? We can only intuit the answer since it is not decreed. This we do know: for the ancient pagan peoples the circle was the most common religious symbol. It often was a feminine sign of vibrancy, pregnancy, and fertility. The ancients often prayed in a circle and sometimes charted the stars from great rock circles. And they were keenly aware of the seasons circling round and round. They built great stone circles still to be seen today. Perhaps the most spectacular ancient circle is to be found at New Grange in County Meath in Ireland. It is estimated to be around four thousand years old.

The circle has many different layers of symbolic meaning. The spheres in the sky were moving about for the ancient peoples. So circles seem to possess great energy. The ancient Druids prayed round and round, *deosil,* in a sun-directed circle. To the present day, so do some Irish Christians. When the early Irish became aware of Jesus, they saw him as a great energetic hero on a grand adventure. And they saw his presence not as static but as dynamic and active everywhere. As Saint Patrick attests: "Christ with me. Christ before me. Christ behind me." So they erected great high crosses with Jesus at the center and the circle all around. Their prayer might well have been:

> O God at the very center
> From whom all being ripples forth,
> Bring us to the circled Celtic cross,
> There to be saved.
> There to be healed.
> There to be enlivened.
>
> *A Contemporary Celtic Prayerbook* [1]

Even today, climb Croagh Patrick the last weekend of July and witness the pilgrims moving in a circular movement around Saint Patrick's Bed. Or go to Saint Brigid's holy well in County Clare and there the shrine itself is arranged in a circular mode and modern pilgrims can be observed moving round and round in a circle as they pray. Their prayer is a "body prayer," in some sense a dance—very Druidic and very Catholic. For somewhere embedded in the Catholic psyche lies the value of body involvement and movement whether in processions or even in some ancient cathedrals through prayerful dance.

Prayer in a dance mode is not some new-age spiritual innovation. It is as old as King David dancing a joyful prayer before the Ark of the Covenant! One Irish writer, Diarmuid O'Murchu, even goes so far as to say that dance was the first human prayer. But dance even precedes the human advent. For dance is the most original and spontaneous expression of joy and exuberance. Anyone who participates in a circle dance knows that there is a special energy to be experienced in the circle. The sum experience is greater than any of its parts.

To dance is to let go and play. Skipping lambs and colts were expressing this delight in the joy of life eons before humans ever moved a foot. Playfulness seems to be a primal blessing and a gift close to the Irish soul. The Irish philosopher Noel Dermot O'Donoghue, in his book *Heaven in Ordinarie*, sees this playfulness as linking all levels of creation. He notes that the playfulness of animals seems startlingly human. Also: "The playfulness of the winds and the flowers is something more than a metaphor. It expresses the freedom and freshness of nature."

Irish Dance

In the twenty-first century, Irish dance and music, whose roots go back to the harp that played through Tara's halls and the itinerant bag pipers who roamed ancient byways, has in this new time seized the world's center stage. Its renaissance fulfills the old Irish adage: "This world will pass away, but love and music will endure."

Tory

So come now with me on a journey to a faraway island and join the dance! Jim Hunter in the University of Ulster Press describes Tory Island as the most remote and exposed to the sea of all the inhabited Irish islands that lie along the Irish coast. Tory is the last inhabited island before Iceland and lies off the extreme northwest coast of Donegal. And down through the ages its music and dance has echoed back from the heights of Mount Frigal across the murmuring sea.

On our way over from Erigal to Tory, Mick Moloney, the Irish folklorist and our group leader, was telling us what to expect: "There are about 140 islanders on Tory—all Irish speaking—but they will be happy to visit with us for they are also bilingual. There are cliffs on the island that rival the Cliffs of Moher. There is also one pub, one church, one tree, and one king! His name is Patsy Dan Rogers and he is the last king remaining in Ireland and his kingship is traced all the way back to the days when Saint Colmcille arrived there in the sixth century."

The islanders are still closely connected to the saint. There is the legend of the Duggan family. It was Duggan who helped Saint Colmcille to land after he had been rejected several times. In return for this, the saint made him king of the island. So Patsy Dan Rogers, the present king, is part of an unbroken line which goes back to the sixth century! And to this family were awarded certain privileges regarding sacred clay trod upon by Saint Colmcille. These are maintained to this present day.

Mick concluded by saying, "Now the islanders are looking forward to a grand party and they will want to dance away the hours." We all chuckled about that—but yes indeed, for two nights in a row—wild Irish step dancing far into the night! And there was Patsy Dan leading the dance. Patsy Dan, a dapper king wearing a Greek fisherman's hat and sporting a gold earring and three gold rings upon his fingers.

When we first arrived on Tory, we were greeted by Patsy Dan, his hand resting on a gold-headed cane shaped like a bird. With typical Irish hospitality he and some of the other islanders escorted us to Hotel Tory, the only local hotel. Remote as it might be, there was nothing backward about the hotel. In fact, some of the best meals we experienced on our trip through Ireland we had there. It was there that we learned that Tory Island derives its name from the high pinnacle cliffs eroded by the battering swells of the Atlantic. Although the hotel is up to date and modern, human habitation on the island is ancient. There were neolithic farmers here four thousand years ago. At one time, Tory Island was occupied by a race of pirates whose God-Chief was Balor of the Evil Eye. Anton Meehan, one of the younger Tory islanders, has painted the resolute Colmcille vanquishing Balor who bears the visage of a fire-breathing dog.

Art on Tory

Tory is a small but mighty island full of surprises. It possesses its own flourishing artist colony, including "himself"—Patsy Dan—plus Michael Finbarr Rogers, Anton Meehan, and Ruari Rogers. These artists have produced the island's own distinctive style of painting known as "primitive art." The Ulster press release about Tory tells a story about Derek Hill, a painter of international recognition who uses Tory as a base for much of his work. On one occasion, he was approached by an islander, Jimmy Dixon, who claimed he could paint as well as Derek Hill. The artist challenged him and offered him art material, paints, and a brush. Jimmy refused the brush, saying he would make his own from hairs of a donkey's tail. As a result, Dixon became the first primitive artist from Tory and with the support of Derek Hill his work is now acclaimed in the art world.

Patsy Dan, as one of the primitive artists, paints the island he knows so well and loves so much. The lighthouse, the helicopter, the boats, the two villages, and the early Christian remains. To the artist's eye of Patsy Dan, Tory is a vibrant mystical and romantic island. When Patsy Dan took his exhibition of Tory paintings to Chicago, over one hundred thousand Americans visited the exhibit.

Precious Jewels

One of the highlights of our stay on Tory was two nights filled with exuberant Irish step dancing. And for me, one of those dancing nights had its preface back on the mainland at Glencolmcille, several nights before we went to Tory. At Glencolmcille, I was standing at the top of a mountain road at twilight. The sheep were grazing on the crown of the hill, a scene of great peace and repose. When I looked down the road toward the ocean shore below, I noticed a small figure in a red jacket coming up the road from the sea. Finally, as she drew closer, I recognized her as Diane, one of the youngest adults from our group of forty. As she approached, her hair, lacking any gray, glistened in the rays of the departing sun. With her red jacket and young looking face, she exuded the vibrancy of a young hiker not tired from the uphill climb. She and I had not had an opportunity to visit and so Diane stopped and we began a conversation.

"Have you been to Ireland before?" I asked.

"Oh yes. Yes, right here—last year, with my husband."

"Oh—your husband could not make the trip this year?"

"No. . . . He died six months ago from melanoma . . . and I have been retracing this journey we made together . . . and it has brought back precious memories—like taking treasured jewels out of a jewel box."

I was stunned by the beauty of her response, and it lingers with me still, "memories like treasured jewels."

A few days later, when we reached Tory Island, Diane entered fully into the spirited Irish step dancing. At one point, in making the circle, she got confused and managed to mess up the set that left everyone scrambling for their place and erupting in laughter. And there she was—the young widow in the red jacket leading the laughter!

As I stood there, I said to myself, "Now here is a truly spirited person, remembering the past, retracing the circle of memories, yet experiencing the breaking of the circle—and still laughing in the midst of chaos! And then moving on with life." When I returned to the United States, I shared this story in a Pentecost homily. A few days later, I received an e-mail from a woman who'd lost two young children to tragic deaths. She let me know how heartening my story was, of Diane, as a spirited person who remembered but also moved on with great courage.

Broken Circles

Perhaps the story of Diane laughing in the broken circle might be a metaphor for all our journeys. Around the Celtic high cross, the circle is perfect and unbroken. And so is God's love for us. But only God forms a perfect circle. On our human journeys, we experience personal broken circles—bereavement, separations, lost friendships, trials, illnesses, and setbacks. In our circle dances of life, these jagged edges and fractures occur in our circles. Chaos and messiness can break the harmony of our circle dances. Perhaps this might be one reason why Irish iconographers are fond of the spiral circle. You see, the spiral is a circle bent out of shape!

The Jagged Edges of Broken Cultural Circles

There are also broken circles in our postmodern culture. Our time, a period of flux and change, would seem to be an age in need of rediscovering the Celtic image of the cross in the circle. We need the energy that flows from the Christ circle and a balanced lifestyle to deal with the jagged edges of brokenness we all experience in one way or another. Among these sharp cultural edges are exhaustion, alienation, rugged individualism, cynicism, and addiction.

Signs of Our Times—The Fracture of Exhaustion

Robert Reich, a former secretary of labor speaking at a gathering in Phoenix, Arizona, pointed to exhaustion as one of the signs of our times. He called attention to two groups in our society who are running on the fast track to the point of exhaustion. One he called the "super fast trackers." These are the folks who are making lots of money fast but are unsure how long that will last since economies and jobs can change so quickly. So they run as fast as they can, making hay while the sun shines, because one never knows whether they might be downsized tomorrow.

The other large group consists of folks who are running as fast as they can and working extra hours just to catch up. Both races can end in exhaustion. Reich pointed out that, at the turn of the twenty-first century, Americans are working longer hours than any other developed country and this would include Japan and Germany.

The Celtic circle around the cross is a holistic image. To lead a holistic life, one must balance work, play, prayer, and leisure. In a classic work, Josef Pieper wrote that leisure is the essential basis for culture. A culture that is based on the premise of working more and more, faster and faster, so that we can buy more and more and have little time left to enjoy what we have is a fractured and jagged culture whose stress will shatter any kind of holistic living. At least in rural Ireland, a more leisurely lifestyle still persists. And one of the reasons Ireland draws so many tourist visitors is precisely the more relaxed lifestyle that allows visiting with neighbors and often not having to open the store until 9:30 or 10:00 in the morning. Visiting Ireland can be a wake-up call for overworked and over-stressed Americans.

The Fracture of Alienation

In chapter two we focused on the separation from the earth that we experience in our modern culture. The circle around the Celtic cross can remind us that we live on an earth circle, are warmed by a sun circle, and sleep beneath a moon circle. The earth itself is girded by a life-giving rainforest circle. When we forget the very ground upon which we stand, we are alienated and disconnected.

Richard Anderson, who lectures in environmental studies at the University of California at Santa Barbara, writes that mankind is experiencing a great grief because of our assault on nature. Some surveys suggest that 80 percent of Americans say that they are concerned about the environment, and that they are somewhat aware of the gravity of the situation but just too busy to let this awareness intrude on their peace of mind. Besides, what can one individual do? As a matter of fact, there is much that an individual can do, as illustrated by the excellent resources published by the Union of Concerned Scientists. [2]

Anderson says that human reactions to ecological despoliation can follow the grief pattern—from denial, to anger, to the despair of "It's too big to solve." It is precisely at this stage of awareness that Christians have a source of energy. For the Christian, trans-formation is always possible. Christ has called us to heal the broken circles and his grace is sufficient.

The ecological problem is at its very root a spiritual problem. The American Catholic bishops have published a pastoral letter regarding global warming in which they teach that "our response to global climate change should be a sign of our respect for God's creation." They also call upon their people and government to "recognize the seriousness of the global warming threat." [3]

Over and over in the ancient prayers of the Celts, we find a connection between nature, prayer, and spirituality. This is a "secret" that needs to be rediscovered in the new century. And we have a beautiful prayer that assures us that with God's help we can and must renew the face of the earth:

Come, Holy Spirit,
fill the hearts of your faithful.
Enkindle in us the fire of your love
and *we shall be recreated*
and you shall renew the face of the earth!

The Christ circle is one of renewable energy, not exhaustion.

The Fracture of Individualism

The cult of the individual creates a lonely road. Liam Treacy, a Servite priest from Dublin, says that it is precisely the Irish gift for community that is needed in our culture. The circle is of course an image of inclusivity and collaboration. When the circle is widened, it is stronger. Perhaps one of the most encouraging signs of our times is the widening of the circle. Right up to the middle of the last century, people were often contained in tight, exclusive circles, ethnic circles, racial circles, sexual circles. It took a black man, Martin Luther King, to really show us what the Celtic cross is all about: Christ at the center of a circle that includes all God's children.

The Cultural Fractures of Cynicism and Addiction

A cynic is a disappointed perfectionist. Could it be that an advertising culture, which tries to tell us that there is a perfect and immediate solution for every problem, will of its very nature lead our young down a path of disappointment? How can one explain that Ireland, a land of beauty that attracted people from around the world at the turn of the century, had an estimated thirteen thousand heroin users and at the turn of this new century needed forty-four drug treatment centers in the Dublin area alone. Of course, this is not just an Irish problem. In upscale Scottsdale where I live, the police just raided a place not too far away where it was suspected that ecstasy was being distributed. In many places ecstasy has become the preferred drug of fifteen- and sixteen-year-olds at all-night Rave dance parties.

Ecstasy

There is a human hunger for "ecstasy." In some way we are wired for it. The seventh secret of the genuine Celtic Spirit—the dance around the cross—is a secret because too many of our youth around the world are led to believe that they can only find ecstasy in drugs and alcohol. The good news that I discovered in traveling around Ireland to music festivals was that a great number of young people are immersed in music and dance and are a part of the great Irish cultural revolution of the Celtic Spirit. They observe the Irish American Michael Flatley, the fastest dancer ever, doing twenty-eight taps per second and this gives great encouragement for youngsters to take up the dance. Travel around Ireland in the spring and attend the various music festivals and you will be enlivened and encouraged by the youth you will see performing.

The End of Celtic Civilization?

Five years after Thomas Cahill wrote *How the Irish Saved Civilization*, Mary Kenny wrote a book about how the Irish lost it! Her book is pretty even-handed and ends on a hopeful note. However, one might infer from it that the younger Irish generation will move further away from their Irish Catholic roots and Celtic spirituality.

Andrew Greeley—the Catholic priest, sociologist and novelist—decided to look into this possibility. In his looking, he unearthed some interesting results. In an article in the March 2001 edition of *America* magazine, Greeley, as only Greeley can, gave a pithy response: "If sex and authority are what Catholicism is about—and many will contend that they are—then the Irish are no longer Catholic. But neither is anyone else."

What Greeley's initial surveys show is that, despite the fact that only seven percent of the age group born in the 1970s had a great deal of confidence in the "church," still 70 percent of them had a high confidence in their local priest! So not only is politics "local," it seems "church" is experienced as local as well. The largest and youngest group of Irish children and teens is most likely to say they are close to Catholicism.

Considering the earthiness of Catholic and local Irish spirituality, Greeley affirms what Rev. David Tracy has said about the essence of Irish religious experience—that it is still based on simple nature mysticism. This data would seem to indicate that the Celtic cross may well remain firmly planted at the grassroots where it has always been. In considering all of this, Fiona's words spoken in Dublin seem pretty accurate: "Celtic spirituality—the young—it's in their bones!"

Closing the Circle

We followed Fiona's advice and circled around Ireland and finally came to Tory, an out-of-the-way place, with one foot faithful to the past Celtic Spirit and the other very much dancing into the present. On the way out to Tory, we passed several islands with deserted old homes, bleak and forlorn, and one could only wonder if, on those cold winter nights when the Atlantic rises and roars, there are ghostly voices there lamenting what once was.

On Tory the natives still endure. Their attachment to their island, which bears the brunt of the Atlantic's rage during the winters, is admirable. In 1974 an Atlantic storm bit and clawed at the island with the rage of Balor. Like an angry dog it would not release its grip. For over eight weeks the island was isolated from the mainland! After that, some families left, but most stayed on.

Caitlin Matthews, in her *Encyclopedia of Celtic Wisdom*, writes that an abiding connection to the land was central to Irish belief. This is so on Tory. The presence of the vivid memory of Saint Colmcille and the islanders' rugged ancestors is almost palpable. Michael Jenner writes that in Ireland, "the ghosts tug at the sleeves of the living." Today, as did their ancestors, the Tory boaters still carry Colmcille's blessed earth in their boats. And Colmcille's sixth-century Tau cross still welcomes visitors as they alight on the island.

Tory's king reverences that past and believes in Tory's future and devotes his energy to saving Tory from evacuation. He says: "May God in heaven help us if we don't win. No matter where you are, the place where you were born and reared is the place you love. We have every right to stay here. We want to stay here and hand it over to future generations."

On one of the dancing nights at Tory, I was standing in the doorway, and the king took a moment out from the frenetic step dancing. On his way through the door he muttered, not to me nor to anyone else nearby, but to the God who hovers close to dancing and joy: "Thank God for everything!"

This exclamation reminded me of what Robert Johnson wrote in his book *He*, that the art of happiness is contentment with what is. He added that, if you cannot be happy with lunch, it is not likely you'll be happy over anything! On Tory, life is simple and the natives know how to dance to the joy of the art of happiness.

There I completed my seventh circle journey around Ireland. In that adventure, and in the six before it, I had journeyed in many ways to the soul of Ireland. I found it on Croagh Patrick in the west, at New Grange in the east, at Patrick's head in the north and Kinsale in the south, and at so many places in between. In many ways, Tory seemed to sum up that indomitable soulfulness of Ireland.

Tory—A Boundary at the Edge

For the ancient Celts, boundaries were important but at certain times and places these boundaries were permeable. At these transit places, as Deidre Clancy writes in her article entitled "Celtic Consciousness," the flux between states of consciousness created the sacred. Thus, powerful was the twilight because it was neither night nor day. Deidre notes that for the ancient Celts there was easy movement between the earth body, the physical spirit, and the radiant soul light. There was no moat dividing body and soul. So it is with Tory. It is neither east nor west. It is the holy portal between.

It rests precariously at the very edge of Europe in the shadow of Mount Erigal and it is at the edge of the venture to the west and another world. Saint Brendan may well have waved goodbye to Europe as he passed on his way to Iceland and as many believed to North America. So a visit to Tory is a pilgrimage to a special place where one can glimpse a

> Last look back at Erin
> At the edge of yesterday
> And all tomorrows.

The Seventh Secret of the Celtic Spirit

The Celtic Spirit that flourishes on Tory is indeed signified by the Celtic cross with Christ at the center and his energy radiating out like the rays of the sun. It means that Christ is indeed everywhere—in the forests and in the seas, at kitchen and hearth, and on the dance floor at Tory where Patsy Dan murmured "Thank God for everything!" as though God was at his elbow. And for the Celts, God is at their elbow!

Mary Aileen Schmmiel writes that John Scotus Eriugena was one of the many wandering Irish theologians who traipsed across Europe with a torch where the light of faith was flickering. He ended up teaching at the Frankish court in the ninth century. He taught that, in a sense, God emptied himself out in creation and remained diffused throughout all created things. Like the pagan Lugh, the light of the long hand, the Christian God was diffused like the sunlight enlightening and warming everything. John

Scotus (the Irishman) taught a theology, not of pantheism but of panentheism, that is, God is in every thing—but God is more than any thing. This is a teaching needed for our times where too often God is sometimes relegated to way up there, or is simply seen as absent and uncaring.

The New Physics

At the beginning of the new century, the new physics has searched deep down and all around. And what has been discovered? That the universe is dancing! The new scientists have discovered that the universe is not some clock whose exact time is predictable. No! There is randomness and unpredictability. Chaos and unexpected convergences occur. There is a mystery deep down and all around. Just as the dancers on Tory made intricate patterns in their step dancing, and just as Diane brought some confusion and chaos, just as the dancers formed a new pattern out of the confusion—so too in the quantum world there are both patterns and confusion! As David Toolen, S.J., writes in his *The Voice of the Hurricane—Cosmology and a Theology of Nature*, the essence of created things reveals that matter/energy is profoundly social!

It would seem that according to process theology, God and the world and creation are all part of an ongoing rather than static process. Rather than a system locked in stone, all of creation is a rolling, flowing stream. Somehow we are all interconnected. There is really no separation between the observer and the observed!

John Scotus Eriugena would have liked this revelation. It reveals a oneness in creation. The old philosophic question of whether there are many or only one would be answered, YES— the many are one and the one are many, and theologically the Spirit of God is present and at work in all. There is a great spiritual energy at work here and it is needed by those who are tired in spirit. It is needed for an ecotheology that sees the created world not just as raw material but as the precious seedbed of God's ongoing creativity.

The Light Blazing Forth from the Circle

The prophetic scientist and French Jesuit spiritual writer Teilhard de Chardin wrote that the great mystery of Christianity is the transparence of God in the universe. He observed the sterility of abstract theology and believed that Christianity must regain its vigor by connecting to the natural aspirations of the earth. He saw science and spirituality converging. He wrote in *The Sense of Man* that the ideas of scientific research and future progress do not eclipse the Christ event. Quite to the contrary, the light of Christ can serve as the central core of progress.

The Core

The "core" is always the center of the circle, just as Jesus is the core, the center of the Celtic cross. David Toolen suggests that the cosmology of Black Elk, the Sioux medicine man, which saw a vision of active interacting circles, may very well be similar to what new physics is telling us. And it is interesting to note that Black Elk's shrine at Blair, Nebraska, features a messianic figure mounted on a Celtic cross with radiating energy flowing out. Teilhard and John Scotus Eriugena would have liked both the vision of Black Elk as well as his shrine. Toward the end of his life, Black Elk was baptized and put Christ at the center of the great circle.

This raises the question as to which Christ we would image in our new century at the center of the Celtic cross. Who is the Christ that we need for our time and our future time? Do we not need . . .

> . . . A *Risen Christ* who is energizing, not constantly expiring?
> . . . A *Quantum Christ* who is deep down and all around?
> . . . A *Healing Christ* who breaks through the bonds of addiction and denial?
> . . . A *Saving Christ* who fills what Richard Rohr calls the "hole in our soul"?
> . . . A *Loving Christ* who is of earth and who blesses our holy grounding?

... A *Teaching Christ* who helps us realize that to be ecological is to be spiritual?

... A *Dynamic Christ* who blesses creativity that births the good, the true and the beautiful?

... A *Carpenter Christ* who presides over our labor, which is the work of God?

... A *Farmer Christ* who blesses a fertile earth and curses only a fruitless fig tree?

... An *Inclusive Christ* whose circle is expanding with the energies of both sexes?

... An *Affirming Christ* who chose women as the first witnesses of the resurrection and wants their voices heard now as then?

... A *Healthy Christ* who is a model of a simpler, holistic lifestyle?

... A *Dancing Christ* who will lead us all the in dance of life?

In Ireland, at Dysart, the Christ figure at the center of the high cross wears a kilt! He looks as if he is ready to come down off that cross and join the Resurrection Dance!

> I danced in the morning when the world was begun,
> And I danced in the moon and the stars and the sun,
> And I came down from heaven
> and I danced on the earth.
> At Bethlehem I had my birth.
> "Dance then, wherever you may be;
> I am the Lord of the Dance, said he.
> I'll lead you all wherever you may be,
> I will lead you all in the dance," said he.
> Shaker Song

Prayer

Christ with me,
Christ before me, Christ behind me.
Christ in me, Christ beneath me, Christ above me.
Christ on my right, Christ on my left,
Christ when I lie down, Christ when I sit down,
Christ when I arise,
Christ in the heart of everyone who thinks of me,
Christ in the mouth of everyone who speaks of me,
Christ in every eye that sees me,
Christ in every ear that hears me.

Saint Patrick's Breastplate

Journal Option:
**The main insights I want to take away from the journey
I have made through this book are . . .**

Notes:

[1] William John Fitzgerald, *A Contemporary Celtic Prayerbook,* ACTA, 1998, cover.

[2] Union of Concerned Scientists, Two Brattle Square, Cambridge MA, 02238-9105, e-mail: ucsusa.org, website: www.ususa.org.

[3] *Global Climate Change: A Plea for Dialogue and the Common Good,* United States Conference of Catholic Bishops, 1-800-235-8722, or www.usccb.org.

The Shadow Side

To see fully,
we must not only
see the face of the sun.
But also the back of the moon.

William Butler Yeats

I n the ebb and flow of history there are low tides and high tides. It is so for every nation, for every tribe, for every culture and every person. There are times when gold seems to appear on the surface and is easily discovered and there are times when it is hidden and must be mined out of grit and gravel. And even on the brightest days there are shadows.

It would be naïve and Pollyannaish in this book to leave the impression that all has been or is glorious with the Irish. The shadow side of the Irish through all the centuries must also be admitted. So yes, Caesar testifies that among the pre-Christian Celts of his time, sometimes captives were placed in wicker baskets and burned as human sacrifices. Heads were taken and prized as trophies. The pre-Christian Celts were fierce and wild, as well as imaginative and spiritual. It is all the more wondrous then that the Christ light came into this darkness and won its victory without any bloodshed!

Down through the centuries, behind the brightness, there was always a shadow side and it crossed the sea into the new world. In the midst of the current Celtic revival in Ireland there are shadows to be acknowledged as well.

Literary Portraits of the Irish

The publication of *Angela's Ashes* by Frank McCourt depicts the travails of one alcohol afflicted family in Limerick during hard times, finding the clergy as uncaring, and the communal life in tatters. Limerick is depicted as a city of gloom and despair. However, Mary Kenney, in her book *Goodbye to Ireland*, disputes this one-sided view that pictures nearly everyone and everything in McCourt's book as nasty and cruel. She claims that most people in Ireland at that time were just the opposite. Quite to the contrary of McCourt's skewered portrait, Mary Kenney writes that the majority of Irish during those poor times shared their poverty with cheerfulness, courage, and wit!

Other literary sources which portray the darker side of Irish life in the last two centuries include Patrick MacGill's *Children of the Dead End* and Nuala O'Faolain's *Are You Somebody? The Accidental Memoir of a Dublin Woman*. MacGill's book paints the hard picture of dirt-poor poverty in nineteenth-century Ireland. It created a sensation in Ireland when published in 1914 and was unsparing in its criticism of some tyrannical Irish priests. And of course Joyce's retreat scene in *The Portrait of an Artist As a Young Man* is memorable. O'Faolain's memoirs, published in 1996, in contrast to McCourt's older memories, presents a more balanced picture of both the bright and the dark sides of growing up Catholic in Dublin. Alice Taylor's *To School Through the Fields* (1988) provides memories of growing up in rural Ireland. Her recollections paint an idyllic portrait that often exemplifies the seven secrets mentioned in this book.

The Current Turn-of-the-Century Irish Republic

What about now? Will the golden glories of the past melt away in the new century? Will modern Erin bury in the past the seven secrets of the Celtic Spirit and all the rest of her unique blessings? Some might think so. Headlines like these from current Irish newspapers are troubling:

> "More than a third of Ireland's sewage is being discharged in an untreated manner" *(Irish Independent)*.

> "Inter-Racial Couple in Center of Dublin Attacked and Stabbed by White Irish Youth" *(Gwynne Dyer, London)*.

> "Irish Gain Reputation as Major Litterbugs in Europe" *(Associated Press)*.

> "Road to Riches or Road to Ruin? The Problems of Land Use, Air Pollution and Immigration Will Test the Irish Soul" *(from Galway by Ronald Bosrock)*.

The Future?

The future is held in the hands of the present majority group in Ireland—her youth. How will the Irish youth respond to such headlines? Esther de Waal, writing a viewpoint article in the *London Tablet* titled, "A Takeover Bid for the Celtic Way," advises Irish youth that the ancient Celtic spirituality offers a holistic spirituality that coincides with the new science they are learning. She also suggests that a return to the kind of Celtic spirituality illustrated in this book and others can become an immensely significant promise for the future provided that "they do not deny the darkness, pain and suffering that is part of the fullness of the Celtic experience."

The Irish American Experience

The history of the vast majority of Irish immigrants in the United States is a glorious story of hard work and success. These new Americans helped to dig the canals and lay the railroad tracks that connected a continent. Many formed regiments of Irish soldiers and fought valiantly for both the North and the South in the Civil War. However, there is a shadow side as well. The darkest moment for the immigrant Irish in America also came during the Civil War. In 1863, mobs of Irish in New York became enraged when the rich were able to buy themselves out of a hitch in the Union Army for three hundred dollars. Irish memories of injustice from their former English overlords surfaced. Their indignation was righteous. The riots that followed were not. Irish mobs surged through the streets of New York. Eighteen innocent Black people were lynched. Total casualties counted two thousand dead.

The Darkest Hours

One of the most even-handed treatments of the Irish American Catholic experience in the United States, and the more recent centuries in Ireland, can be found in Timothy Joyce's *Celtic Christianity, A Sacred Tradition, A Vision of Hope.* He calls the most recent centuries the darkest hours for the Irish. He describes these later Irish as a "paradoxical people" cut off from their earlier Celtic-influenced Catholic roots, and too often prone to alcohol abuse because of the presence of so much pain and suffering. He also points out that in the darkest hours there were also glimmers of light.

The Best of Times and the Worst of Times

Looking over the long span of history, in both the best and the worst of times, it seems that it has always been possible to mine for Celtic gold. In MacGill's autobiographical novel, a lad whose formal education ended at age ten must leave home and emigrate to the mines of Scotland, and yet he still possesses the vivid Celtic imagination and is able to spin a story as well as any seanachie ever did. He writes lyrical and haunting words about the enchantment of the land and the dearness of the earth beneath his feet:

> It was the night of many winds beating against the bald peaks that thrust their pointed spires into the mystery of the heavens. From time to time, I could hear the falling earth as it was loosened from its century-long resting place and flung heavily into the womb of some fathomless abyss. God was still busy with the work of creation! [1]

And God still is. Whether from the pens of the ancient scribes of Iona or the novels of the present age, there is still something quite beautiful about the Celtic Spirit that so far continues to sparkle even in the midst of grit and gravel.

Notes: [1] Patrick MacGill, *Children of the Dead End*, Birlinn Limited, 5 New Street, Edinburgh, Scotland, 1999, p. 177.